NEW PERSPECTIVES FOR US-ASIA PACIFIC SECURITY STRATEGY

The 1991 Pacific Symposium

NEW PERSPECTIVES FOR US-ASIA PACIFIC SECURITY STRATEGY

The 1991 Pacific Symposium

Edited by
Dora Alves

1992

 National Defense University Press
Washington, DC

National Defense University Press Publications

To increase general knowledge and inform discussion, NDU Press publishes books on subjects relating to US national security.

Each year, in this effort, the National Defense Univerity, through the Institue for National Strategic Studies, hosts about two dozen Senior Fellows who engage in original research on national security issues. NDU Press publishes the best of this research.

In addition, the press publishes other especially timely or distinguished writing on national security, as well as new editions of out-of-print defense classics, and books based on University-sponsored conferences concerning national security affairs.

Opinions, conclusions, and recommendations expressed or implied within are solely those of the authors and do not necessarily represent the views of the National Defense University, the Department of Defense, any other US Govenment agency, or any agency of a foreign government.

NDU Press publications are sold by the U.S. Government Printing Office. For ordering information, call (202) 783-3238, or write to: Superintendent of Documents, US Government Printing Office, Washington, DC 20402.

First printing, May 1992

Library of Congress, Cataloging-in-Publication Data

Pacific Symposium (National Defense University) (12th : 1991)
   New perspectives for US-Asia Pacific security strategy : the 1991
Pacific Symposium / edited by Dora Alves.
      p. cm.
   Includes bibliographical references.
   1. Pacific Area—National security—Congresses. 2. Asia—National
security—Congresses. 3. United States—National security
—Congresses. 4. Pacific Area—Military relations—United States
—Congresses. 5. United States—Military relations—Pacific Area
—Congresses. 6. Asia—Military relations—United States
—Congresses. 7. United States—Military relations—Asia
—Congresses. I. Alves, Dora. II. Title. III. Title: New perspectives for United States-
Asia Pacific security strategy.
UA830.P37   1991
355'.033'01823—dc20   91-45953
                                                                 CIP

CONTENTS

AUSTRALIA AND THE SOUTH PACIFIC

MAPS

TABLES

CHARTS

FOREWORD

As with previous volumes based on annual Pacific Symposia, these papers constitute an authoritative assessment of recent trends affecting security, social, and political conditions and the economies of the Pacific region. Presented as the Gulf War was ending, Eastern Europe was undergoing major changes, and the US recession was causing international concern, the papers examine new security strategies in the Asia-Pacific region.

Beginning with a *tour d'horizon* of regional developments as seen by the Commander-in-Chief of the US Pacific Command, the collection examines such general issues as the progress of democratization, the effects of new technology, and the changing role of the military in Pacific nations. Other papers look at more specific issues like the future of China-Japan and US-Japan relations, prospects for reunification of the Koreas, and Australian strategic requirements.

The sudden end of the Cold War has had a discernible effect on the strategic thinking of Pacific nations. During the symposium, several speakers suggested that the old strategic balance dependent on military—especially nuclear—force might be replaced by one in which international institutions play a more powerful role. Others explored ways in which nations formerly protected by the US nuclear umbrella could become more self-reliant, reducing the burden on the United States. In everyone's mind was the example of the United States and the Soviet Union working together after four decades of enmity. Many participants believed that this example had already contributed toward a reduction of tensions between China and Vietnam, between the Koreas, and between the new Russia and the Republic of Korea.

As the host for the Pacific Symposia, the National Defense University is especially gratified that this forum continues to produce the interchange of ideas it was intended to foster.

J. A. BALDWIN
Vice Admiral, US Navy
President, National Defense
University

PREFACE

National Defense University's 1991 Pacific Symposium took place as a new approach to global security was emerging. Superpower *confrontation* was losing sway as the organizing principle while—in the wake of the international effort in the Persian Gulf war—the incentive toward *cooperation* in regional and global security concerns was gaining momentum. Such cooperation could be seen in the Asia-Pacific region, where old adversaries, as well as old friends, are slowly building multidimensional linkages of mutual benefit. Interdependence is, little by little, fostering a common security approach, an approach which encompasses security in all its multiple facets.

The papers selected for this anthology touch, as do previous volumes, on a wide range of multilateral issues that confront this region of so many different social systems and cultural values. As Secretary of Defense Dick Cheney said in Tokyo shortly before the symposium got underway in Hawaii, the United States presence in the region, supported by alliances, can provide a "balancing wheel" for Asia-Pacific countries adjusting to the new security environment.

NDU Press acknowledges with gratitude the work of Dr. Harold W. Holtzclaw, organizer of this and several earlier Pacific Symposia until his recent retirement. His skill in selecting authors and participants ensured informative, stimulating discussions, the essence of which could then be preserved in the series of Pacific volumes with the familiar cover. We also thank his able administrative staff for their unflagging support.

THE EDITOR

NEW PERSPECTIVES FOR US-ASIA PACIFIC SECURITY STRATEGY

The 1991 Pacific Symposium

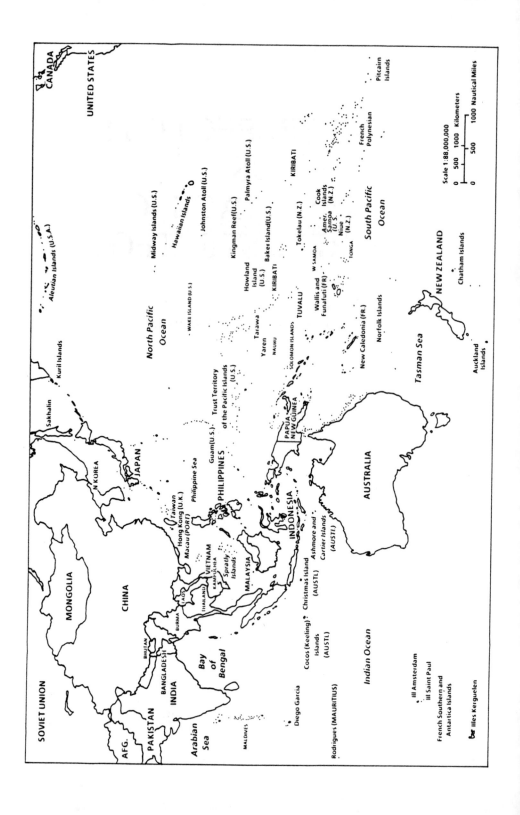

Keynote Address:
NEW PERSPECTIVES ON ASIA AND THE PACIFIC

Admiral Charles R. Larson

Admiral Charles R. Larson *received his fourth star in February 1990 when he became Commander in Chief, US Pacific Fleet. The admiral graduated with distinction from the US Naval Academy, served as a naval aviator, and was later accepted for nuclear power training. He served in two fleet ballistic submarines and as executive officer of a nuclear attack submarine before being selected as the first naval White House Fellow. Before reporting back to sea duty he served as special assistant to the Secretary of the Interior and as naval aide to the President. Subsequently, he became Commander, Submarine Development Group 1, Director of the Strategic Submarine Division and Trident Coordinator on the staff of the Chief of Naval Operations. Admiral Larson has also served as Director, Long Range Planning, Commander Submarines Mediterranean (NATA), Superintendent of the Naval Academy, Commander Striking Fleet Atlantic/Commander Second Fleet, and Deputy Chief of Naval Operations for Plans, Policy, and Operations.*

I'm very pleased that my first official duty as CINC is to offer you PACOM's perspective on this region and the future. Of course, gaining a "new perspective" requires more than just viewing from a different angle. Perspective implies depth and reflection—and that requires a look backward as well as forward. The past two years have brought the most rapid changes and profound transformations in my lifetime. Despite the fact that it's early in the "New World Order," I think we can identify some lessons from these changes. And from these lessons we can project forward to draw some tentative conclusions—about the direction the future is likely to take; and about how we must influence that direction, if our nation is to survive and prosper.

The first lesson of the recent past is that changes in the world are still working largely in our favor. That is sometimes hard to remember when television offers us pictures of a new crisis every day. But the fact remains that the world is *fundamentally* different today—and *fundamentally* better—than a few short months ago. The major change—and this hasn't been said nearly enough—is the collapse of Communism as a moral force, which brought about the end of the Cold War.

I am talking about more than just changes in the Soviet Union—I'll get to that in a minute. I am referring to the very public bankruptcy of a philosophy that served as a rallying point for disaffected groups all over the world, and provided a serious and continuing threat to our nation, our friends, and our allies. It was this philosophy that split the world into two camps, inspired Communist nations in their quest for expansion, and supported military competition on a global scale.

The beauty of our containment strategy—and its ultimate success—lay in the fact that it let Communism fail on its own. The system that rivaled ours for the souls of developing nations simply didn't work. It was this recognition of failure that drove Gorbachev to *perestroika* and *glasnost,* undermined the support of communist insurgencies, and reduced the threat of a short notice global conflict to its lowest level in two generations. The impact of these changes is evident in many ways: in Soviet cooperation as we forged a UN response to Iraqi aggression; in their gradual withdrawal of offensive forces from Cam Rahn Bay; in their pursuit of warmer diplomatic relations with Japan and the Republic of Korea; and in their exchange of Pacific fleet visits to San Diego and Vladivostok.

It isn't just the Soviets who have changed: it's the world. Some Communist governments may remain powerful or even dangerous, but the image of the workers' paradise has been shattered forever. The bipolar world ended when one of the poles ceased to be attractive, even to its own people. And the changes which produced this multipolar world offer us a multitude of opportunities.

Two years ago a famous article in the *Atlantic Monthly* argued that we have reached "the end of history." It was wrong. But despite the inaccuracy of his catchy title, the author's more subtle suggestion, that the demands of common people are moving the world steadily toward democracy and free market economies, does have merit. And this marks another positive change which we ought to recognize and capitalize upon. Especially in the PACOM area of operations, nations are beginning to see that the solutions for many of their problems lie in economic growth—the kind of growth possible only in free nations.

I think the dramatic success of Japan, and the "Four Tigers," and the new tier of nations coming on behind them speaks volumes about the connection between free government and economic progress. People everywhere want the benefits of our economic system. They see that progress is fostered by private ownership and individual choice. And once granted, those economic freedoms inevitably lead to demands for new political freedoms as well. Nobody is looking to Cuba, Albania, or Vietnam for a model anymore.

That does not mean that every government will eventually look like ours. The enormous diversity of this region will lead to diverse political solutions as well. For example:

- Nepal will hold elections in May but retain its king;

- Many of the dozen South Pacific nations born in the past 15 years are weaving democratic methods into their existing cultural fabric;

- South Korean liberalization is affected by its unique history and the shadow of northern aggression;

- Indonesia, set for rapid expansion with its energetic and hard working population, will develop in line with its strong Muslim heritage;

- and India, the world's largest democracy, will continue to be influenced by the religious and cultural diversity of its population.

The broad movement toward free markets and freer governments gives us new opportunities to establish common interests in this theater while advancing our democratic values at the same time. It also highlights another major change working in our favor—the rising dependence of many nations on international trade.

Simply put, the nations of Asia and the Pacific—and that includes the United States—need each other. We all need uninterrupted access to markets and resources, and we need the regional stability which makes that access possible. This new interdependence works in our favor because it pushes us all toward international cooperation, while offering a golden opportunity to advance US principles and secure US interests—and that's a very positive development indeed.

If one lesson of the recent past is that many changes are working in our favor, another lesson is that sweeping changes are far from over, and the world remains a dangerous place. Demographic changes in this region suggest a trend of rising social pressures. Population growth is accelerating in many areas, threatening to reverse the progress against hunger made in the Green Revolution of a few years ago. India could well overtake China as the world's most populated nation in a generation, and more than half of Filipinos are under the age of 17. In Japan, the trend is exactly the opposite where a graying population will require increasing social services even as the percentage of taxpaying workers declines. And throughout the region, urbanization, with all its attendant problems, is taking place at a remarkable rate. We are used to thinking of urban problems in countries like Japan where Tokyo's density is 10 times that of Washington, DC. But urbanization even affects places like Nepal, where one in 15 of the nation's residents lives in Kathmandu, and the Marshall Islands, where 20,000 people inhabit less than four square miles in the capital city. And even the emerging economic powers face such problems. Many of Bangkok's seven million people, for instance, live in areas where water and sewer systems simply cannot be built.

Changes in the old bipolar order also provide new openings for new demands by ethnic groups, nationalists, and religious extremists. These forces have spurred clashes in Kashmir, Punjab, Sri Lanka, and Papua New Guinea—and they remain a concern in many ASEAN countries.

Meanwhile, the same economic changes that promise to open the door for cooperation, can create tensions as well. Pressures for resources and economic growth are already causing competition between those who are growing economically and jealousies from those who are not. Remember that one of Iraq's major complaints with Kuwait was that the wealth under Kuwaiti soil was not being shared "equally" within the region. Then look to the Spratley Islands with its oil and gas reserves, its overlapping claims, and extensive military construction. Regional tensions also exist over fishing rights and logging techniques, and even water. For example, Vietnamese officials have expressed concerns over Thai plans to irrigate the Mekong River basin at the expense of users downstream.

Clearly, some of the economic changes which we hope will pull the region together could have the opposite effect instead. One of the lessons we can already draw from the conflict in the Mideast is that because of the growing interdependence of economics, even regional conflicts have global implications. Given this increasing importance of regional stability and the growing list of regional irritants, I do not find long-term military trends reassuring. The major change in this regard over the past few years has been the growing range, accuracy, and lethality of conventional weapons, and their proliferation among nations and groups and regimes who may not be responsible members of the world community.

Now there is nothing wrong with any nation having the means to defend itself. In fact, a keystone of our approach to Pacific security has been assisting and encouraging our friends and allies in developing adequate self-defense capabilities. Japan is a good example: by developing the capability to defend her sea lines of communication out to 1,000 miles in close cooperation with US forces, the Japanese help to anchor the security of all Northeast Asia. In Southeast Asia, the ASEAN nations have met with similar success, looking beyond their differences and contributing to the regional stability which encouraged such phenomenal economic growth.

As a result of enormous Third World expenditures on weapons, we enter this new age with the potential for even local conflicts to become lethal, costly, and destructive. Again, Iraq has demonstrated this fact clearly. A nation of only 17 million persons—and one madman—it fielded the fourth largest standing army in the world, and precipitated a crisis that has caused untold human suffering and already cost the world nearly 60 billion dollars, not counting ecological damage and trade losses. Iraq's buildup may be an extreme case, but it is not unique. Even excluding traditional world powers, 20 nations can field more than 1,000 tanks each. Forty-one countries now have diesel attack submarines, and more than 400 submarines are available to nations besides the United States and the USSR.

Weapons of mass destruction have achieved similar popularity. More than two dozen nations boast ballistic missiles, and nearly 30 nations are suspected of conducting research for nuclear or chemical capabilities. Even the *rumor* of nuclear development can be used in an attempt to intimidate neighbors, as we have seen in North Korea. Virtually any plant which produces chemical fertilizer can be modified to turn out nerve gas. More ominous still is renewed discussion of biological weapons. In theory, anyone who can produce a vaccine can produce a disease as well. These dangerous military trends are accompanied by the continuing threat of international terrorism, which can quickly spill across borders to affect regions and nations far from the site of the conflict.

Against this background of dangerous military changes, we should remember that Soviet military capability has not disappeared—it has changed, but it has not gone away. The Cold War didn't end because the Soviets put down their weapons; in fact, they have not done so today. It ended when they gave up trying to export their political dogma to instigate revolution abroad. It was a change in will and intent, not in capability, which in many respects remains as strong as ever.

Soviet military power remains formidable—in fact, it constitutes the Soviet Union's only claim to superpower status. Soviet military spending is higher now than when President Gorbachev came to power, while our "real spending" for defense will fall next year to the lowest level since 1983. Especially in the Pacific theater, the Soviets are replacing quantity with quality, and their capability continues to grow. The question, of course, is whether their nation will return to the "bad old days" of using its military as the dominant instrument of foreign policy.

After hosting sailors of the Soviet Pacific Fleet in San Diego and visiting Vladivostok myself last fall, I am convinced that Soviet citizens want peace and prosperity as much as we do. But prudence demands that we watch their massive force closely. For, as Secretary Baker said in congressional testimony last month, "We cannot rule out the possibility that matters may still turn more for the worse."

So in developing a new perspective on Asia and the Pacific—in examining the changes and the lessons and the trends in the region—I see a future which is:

- less threatening but more volatile;

- less predictable, but more interrelated;

- and less stable, but more dependent on stability than ever before.

It won't be a perfect world, but it will be marked by opportunities for cooperation and progress. And when you compare this with the dangerous global tensions of the past forty years, it looks downright attractive. The key to international security and our own national interests is going to be regional stability.

Without it, the "New World Order" will rapidly become "The New World Disorder."

To promote regional stability when possible and prevail in regional conflict when necessary, the United States must remain regionally engaged. Yesterday, in his change of command remarks, my predecessor, Admiral Hunt Hardisty, said,

> The United States is not the world's policeman, and we do not wish to be. But when an outlaw threatens the entire community, and it's time to round up a posse, it's only right that the leading citizens should volunteer.

We cannot enjoy both the advantages of leadership and the luxury of isolationism.

I am happy to say that the Pacific Command has learned these lessons and put them to use. Today, in the face of what Colin Powell calls the "enduring realities" of continued Soviet military power, vital US interests overseas, and the uncertain course of world events, our Pacific strategy focuses on maintaining regional stability through access, influence, and deterrence.

We are accomplishing this strategy by maintaining trained and ready forward-deployed military forces in theater, and by using them to establish a network of military to military relationships with others. This network is supported by a variety of military programs ranging from major planning and operational exercises like "Team Spirit" in Korea and "Cope Thunder" in the Philippines, to small unit deployments, military personnel exchanges, ship visits—and even the Foreign Military Sales program. This strategy is working today, promoting stability and cooperation throughout our theater. It's a strategy which will work for tomorrow as well.

Of course, we will see some adjustments in force levels in the Pacific. Given the changes in budget realities and the improvements in our strategic relationship with the Soviet Union, the Secretary of Defense has announced a 25 percent reduction in the US military over the next five years, and we are going to take our fair share. Some adjustments have already begun:

- 15,000 personnel will be moving out of Korea, Japan, and the Philippines in the next two years;

- the B-52s are already gone from Guam, we are consolidating operations at some air bases in Korea, and the F-4s will be phased out of Clark Air Force Base by next fall.

In the end we will be a leaner force, principally maritime, with a smaller number of forward deployed air and ground forces, and reinforcements concentrated in Hawaii and Alaska. But it will continue to be a high quality force, adequate to preserve stability, encourage democracy, and deter aggression in this theater.

In short, from my perspective I see a bright future for US security, interests, and ideals, reinforced and advanced by our military strategy in the Pacific. No doubt we will face a host of challenges, but I am confident that we have learned the key lessons of this new world already. We will remain committed to our interests, our allies, and our friends. And because of that commitment, we can look forward to a promising tomorrow.

TOWARD DEMOCRATIZATION AND STABILITY IN ASIA

Dr. Robert A. Scalapino

Dr. Robert A. Scalapino received his B.A. degree from Santa Barbara College and his M.A. and Ph.D. Degrees from Harvard University. He has recently retired from the Political Science Department at Berkeley where he was Robson Research Professor of Government and Director of the Institute of East Asian Studies. Dr. Scalapino is the editor of **Asian Survey** and the author of some 300 articles and 27 books or monographs on Asian politics and US Asian policy. He has traveled extensively in Asia and the Pacific. Dr. Scalapino was a visiting lecturer at Beijing University in 1981 and 1985 and has visited the Soviet Union on eight occasions.

Since the term "democracy" is coveted by every nation from Albania to Zimbabwe, we should make clear our definition of that word at the outset. Stated simply, democracy requires two conditions: genuine political competition in an inclusive political system in which the citizenry have the full rights of participation; and the requisite freedoms of speech, press, organization, assemblage, and religious belief to make participation and choice meaningful.

Freedom can never be absolute. Long ago, an eminent US Supreme Court justice asserted that there should be no freedom to shout "Fire!"in a crowded theater. There will always be vigorous debate in an open society as to where the boundaries of permissibility should be drawn. Most individuals would assert that to engage in violence in the course of protest is not a legitimate exercise of free speech. But issues like this must be decided by the courts in a democratic society, not by administrative fiat.

Democracy is at root a political term. There has long been a serious controversy as to whether that term should include economic and social components. Many socialists have insisted that a pledge of minimum livelihood for citizens, such additional rights in the economic field as the right to employment, and social equality are essential conditions of democracy. It is true that an impoverished, illiterate people may be able to express their desires only inadequately even if given full political freedom. But the case of India illustrates the fact that even in situations where poverty and illiteracy are serious problems, an electorate can register its dissatisfaction by ousting those in power if given the chance, and in the long run, such a possibility is conducive to making those who wield power hold authority more accountable, whatever the defects in the political system. In a democracy, leaders who fail in the tasks of development will sooner or later lose power.

It is important to understand the great philosophic divide that separates Marxism-Leninism and liberalism. The Marxists believe in the perfectibility of a class—the proletariat —and hence, of the individuals who purport to represent that class. Thus, although they may talk about "socialist legalism," basically, they are not concerned with limitations on power. Liberals believe that there is a quotient of evil in all individuals and hence, that power must always be controlled by law and other restraints such as institutional checks and balances.

In this context, let me draw up a balance-sheet on the progress of democracy in Asia and the obstacles or threats that it faces. Let me make it clear at the beginning that the democratic system can and will take many forms, influenced by factors of culture, timing, stage of economic development, and geopolitical circumstances. There is not now, nor will there ever be a single democratic system.

Having made this point, however, it is also important to note that one of the factors that have played a major role in the advances of Asian democracy since World War II has been the existence of a political model in the advanced Western world that had ideological appeal, especially to the elites of nations emerging from colonialism. Much has been made of the appeal of Marxism to such elites, and it is true that the Leninist model attracted a great many Asians during the postwar struggle for independence and development. But it should not be overlooked that in those parts of Asia that had been under British and American rule, significant portions of the elite had been exposed directly or indirectly to democratic values, even if, paradoxically, they were not practiced in the colonies (the Philippines excepted).

British and American tutelage played a very large role in establishing the democratic system throughout much of Asia —from India to Korea and Japan. To be sure, in the latter countries, quite different in their modern histories, American tutelage came in concentrated form, with the imposition of parliamentarism upon an occupied people. Yet here too, through earlier cultural contacts (in the case of Korea) and a parliamentary heritage (in the case of Japan), the prior influence of Western liberalism could be found.

It is vitally important to note, however, that in the first experiments, democracy failed in a number of Asian societies. Generally, the course in such states was toward military rule, as was the case in Pakistan, Burma, Indonesia, and South Korea among others. To explore the reasons for failure is to reveal some of the continuing uncertainties about the future of democracy. In the first place, if political divisions are centrally based upon religious, ethnic, or regional lines, the democratic system is vitiated, and the resulting instability soon creates a sharp aversion to the system, not only from elites but from the grass-roots citizenry as well. It should be remembered that the first priority in the early postwar era was nation-building. This required unity among peoples who in many cases had been subjected to the "divide and rule" principle as practiced by colonial governors. Thus, if democracy served to perpetuate and even exacerbate divisions, it was certain to face rising opposition.

Moreover, as is well known, democracy requires all parties to play by rather complex but supremely important rules. Those who govern must not silence opponents as long as they are operating in accordance with the law, and correspondingly, opponents must accept the legitimacy of the government as long as it was chosen in a fair and legal manner. In addition, while consensus is often desirable, the majority has the right to prevail in case of disagreement so long as minority rights are preserved. And in the final analysis, government by law rather than by "wise men" must be the commanding rule. Yet all of these principles in varying degree run counter to the political culture of Asian societies. It is thus not surprising that democracy acquired an unsavory reputation in many societies during the early years after 1945. Nor have the problems connected with the nature of these societies and their political heritage disappeared.

There was a second powerful reason for the demise of democracy in many parts of Asia in the first decades after World War II. A combination of political instability and the absence of effective economic policies served to retard the development of all but a handful of Asian states. Meanwhile, more disciplined societies such as those under Leninist systems were mobilizing manpower and resources, and with specific economic plans, were showing major gains in productivity, especially in heavy industry. The Stalinist economic model appeared to be working. Thus, China spurted ahead in its first years of Communist rule, and North Korea outdistanced South Korea in the initial years after the Korean War. Having proven that Leninism provided the ideological and organizational weapons for a successful revolution, the Communists seemed to possess a successful post-revolution economic strategy as well.

As events turned out, however, most of the failed democracies of Asia did not take the Leninist path. Rather, they pursued a course that I have labelled authoritarian-pluralism. Politics turned authoritarian, with mass participation restricted, with military or quasi-military rule in effect, and with political freedoms limited, albeit, not usually as severely as in the Leninist states. Yet in the social realm, such institutions as those pertaining to education, religion, and the family operated with a considerable degree of autonomy from the state (although variations occurred both from society to society, and from time to time). And in the economic realm, the market played a vitally important role, even though the state served as planner, guide, and supporter via neomercantilist policies.

Thus, three separate socio-political systems emerged in Asia shortly after World War II, and they continue to the present: Leninist, authoritarian-pluralist, and democratic. However, the relative performance of these systems has undergone various transformations in recent years. It is now universally acknowledged that the Stalinist economic strategy reached a point of diminishing returns long ago, and has displayed increasing defects in recent decades. Even in the Leninist motherland, elites realized the grave problems as early as the Khrushchev era, and indeed, Khrushchev himself searched vainly for remedies. The economic disasters in China such as the commune system and the Great Leap Forward were man-made, but in the post-Mao era, Chinese elites also came to realize the need for a major systemic overhaul. Later, Mongolia was first to follow and then to make the effort to go ahead of its long-time mentor, the USSR. And even the Vietnamese leadership, while divided, has had to contemplate substantial economic reforms in the wake of dismal performance, with Cambodia and Laos pursuing a similar path. Only North Korea has been reluctant to act boldly, fearing the political repercussions. But its poor economic performance in recent years dictates a change, the only questions being when and how. A similar prediction can be made about Burma (now Myanmar), a crypto-Leninist state that has managed to combine hard authoritarianism and economic ineptitude in remarkable degree.

The central problems now confronting the Asian Leninist states are first, how to combine satisfactorily a command and market economy, and second, how to effect economic change without undermining a political system which appears to provide stability to societies that have known deep divisions. Neither problem is easy to resolve. No Leninist state, West or East, has yet been successful in creating a mixed economy on a socialist base, although a number of different experiments are proceeding and perhaps gains will be scored.

Meanwhile, the commitment to political Leninism remains strong in Asia, in contrast to the situation in East Europe. Why? In part, because of the differences in political culture. It should never be forgotten that East Europe and Russia have partaken of the great philosophic, religious, and political traditions of the West even if they have been on its peripheries. Moreover, as has been frequently pointed out, Communism in Europe is associated with Soviet imposition, whereas despite the important Soviet role in implanting Communism in Asia, that movement has also been associated with liberation from Western, Japanese, or Chinese control, hence, with patriotism.

Current trends within Asian Leninist states, however, are inexorably building toward recurrent political crises. It is impossible to create an increasingly open economy and maintain a closed polity. Asian Leninist leaders may charge that "imperialists" are seeking to undermine socialism by "peaceful evolution" but, in fact, it is they who are unconsciously undermining socialism in its Leninist form by effecting economic changes that will progressively challenge the old political order.

It would be wrong to assume, however, that these states— or most of them at least—will be pulled into the democratic orbit. Despite the desires of a small band of intellectuals, neither the leadership nor the citizenry is prepared for, or committed to such a course. Far more likely is the movement of the Asian Leninist states into the category of authoritarian-pluralist societies. Why? Because this is a system that has a greater degree of compatibility with the culture and present stage of development of those societies, and because it has a track record of considerable success.

Most (but not all) of the states following the authoritarian-pluralist path have done well, and some have done exceedingly well. The combination of political stability, often enforced by repressive means, and economic policies well suited both to domestic capacities and the international environment proved a highly effective combination. One need only examine the economic record of South Korea and Taiwan in the decades of the 1960s and 1970s to find evidence of this fact. Indonesia, another society in the same basic political category, has had more mixed results, but its record in recent times has been relatively good. And in South Asia, Pakistan has enjoyed sustained economic growth.

Unlike the Leninists, leaders in most authoritarian-pluralist societies never claimed that their system was the final answer, the ultimate goal. On the contrary, they acknowledged that as development occurred, the political system would evolve. It is true that like all leaders, very few authoritarian power-holders gave up their positions voluntarily. Multiple pressures were generally required, and on occasion, violence. But the greatest pressure lay in the process of development itself. In the most successful authoritarian-pluralist societies, rapid economic growth led to the emergence of a literate, relatively comfortable urban middle-class—using that term loosely. Increasingly, that class sought greater political involvement and demanded greater political openness. Thus, South Korea, having slipped back from democracy in the 1960s and 1970s, undertook its restoration in the 1980s, albeit, not without considerable political turmoil. In Taiwan, Chiang Ching-kuo wisely prepared the way for a political transition just prior to his death. The political system of Thailand evolved in the direction of parliamentarism although even now, the military seek to serve as extra-parliamentary "guardians of the public weal" on occasion. Pakistan and Bangladesh, meanwhile, each in its own way, stand at a political crossroads, with parliamentarism at least partially restored after lengthy periods of military rule.

With the exception of Bangladesh, the move toward greater political openness owes much to socio-economic developments, as has been indicated. Yet one cannot ignore another factor: the influence of the broad external trends in an age when the information-communication revolution is bringing world events into the homes—and the consciousness—of an ever larger number of people. Yet another means of control, namely, isolation, is being removed, and when comparisons can be made, the desire for an alternative considered better grows.

One sees the effect of the communications revolution in more respects than the political. Note the emergence of a cosmopolitan culture, especially among the more educated, economically benefited urban younger generations of Asia. In music, dress, cuisine, and general life-style, they are mixing the former ways of their society with a universal course, sometimes to the consternation of their elders, and in the case of the Leninist states, their political leaders.

Meanwhile, a few Asian states have now maintained democracy for a sufficient period of time to acculturate several generations politically. One such state is Japan. In common with certain other Asian democratic states in Asia, notably Singapore and Malaysia, power at the national level has remained in the same party's hands at the national level in recent decades despite the existence of a high degree of political openness and competitive elections. When one party knows only how to govern and the others know only how to oppose, neither can be fully responsible—and there is evidence of the hazards of continuous rule in each of the countries mentioned above. Nevertheless, the party in power wins because the electorate in these societies is generally satisfied with its policies or not sufficiently dissatisfied to entrust the opposition with power. In any case, the "one and one-half party system" under which these democracies have operated has ensured a degree of stability combined with freedom that might not otherwise have been possible.

In certain other Asian democracies, power at the national level has changed hands through elections. India and Sri Lanka are examples. Through this process, it can be argued, all major elements in the political system have acquired greater understanding, and greater allegiance to that system, even the mainstream Marxist-Leninists. At the same time, the instability that has ensued has been troublesome, especially in India.

Today, India faces some of the most serious political difficulties since independence. Some would assert that the democratic system itself is in jeopardy. Weak leadership, undisciplined parties, and inadequate economic policies have combined with growing ethnic, caste, and religious fissures to produce a grave crisis. The weakness of the center in itself is not wholly a negative factor. That weakness has enabled the more dynamic states within India to move ahead without undue centrist interference. Yet the uncertainties surrounding national policies, and the fluid local-state-national relationships constitute a destabilizing force.

No continent-sized state, to be sure, can avoid the complications of its proportions. Witness the current crisis in the USSR, and a similar, if somewhat less tense, situation in China. To devise a politically acceptable, economically sound federalist structure is an imperative for such states, and one made vastly more difficult when ethnic and sub-cultural differences run deep. Observe the problems that the United States faced in the first two centuries of its existence, and indeed, continues to confront. And yet, the American problem pales in comparison with that facing the Soviet Union, the world's last great empire, or India which has its own imperial remnants, as does China.

We are witnessing the rise of Hindu fundamentalism in India in response to issues like Kashmir and the militancy of certain Islamic elements. And in Sri Lanka, religion combines with ethnicity to fuel a savage civil war. Indeed, throughout most of southern Asia, including its southeast portions, religious, ethnic, and sub-cultural divisions are deeply imbedded. It might be argued, indeed, that the recent trend has been toward their intensification. Nor is this trend unique to East and South Asia.

Why has religion, and especially fundamentalist religion, reentered politics on a global scale and with renewed force? Fundamentalist Islam, Christianity, Judaism, and Hinduism— even Buddhism—are playing important political roles in many parts of the world, long after social scientists declared them passé in the political arena. The principal reason is that secular leaders have generally downgraded ideology, using pragmatic approaches to problem solving, especially given the new priority accorded economics. Even the Leninists have tended in this direction despite recurrent rhetorical flourishes. But people need values, especially in a revolutionary age when one's moorings seem to be threatened by the turbulence of constant and massive change. Religion moves in to fill the vacuum, sometimes with great seriousness of purpose and dedication, sometimes as a force manipulated by political opportunists. In any case, whether an open political system can handle the diversity, and more important, the intolerance of religious, ethnic, and social forces characteristic of certain states and regions, remains a question. Having analyzed the factors that have forwarded the democratic movement in Asia and weakened the Leninist order, we are brought to focus on the challenges confronting democracy as we move into the final decade of the twentieth century.

Those who have proclaimed the death of Leninism and the triumph of liberalism are only half right at best. Indeed, it does appear that Leninism in its Stalinist form at least cannot be resuscitated. Yet as we have noted, it is very likely that a number of the old Leninist states—and others as well—will find the authoritarian-pluralist model more compatible with their nature and needs than the liberal pattern. Moreover, democratic states, including those of the advanced, industrial West, face certain new challenges that have not yet been seriously confronted. Unfortunately, it is virtually taboo to discuss some of the problems that confront us.

Let us take the role of the media in a free society. It is recognized that a free media is a requisite of democracy. Yet is it acknowledged that today, the media have become a part of governance? The media plays an equal or more powerful role than elected officials in shaping and changing public opinion, and in a democratic society, public opinion in the final analysis is the decisive factor in the capacity to govern. The central problem with the media is not political bias, although that exists. The key problem is the penchant for sensationalism, especially in the electronic media, and hence, the lack of balance. That which is gradual, developmental, and complex gets short shrift. As a result, our informational diet is heavily laden with crises and extremities of various sorts. To question the media's role is to bring down upon one's head charges of McCarthyism or suppression of free speech. But with freedom must go responsibility.

Yet another problem lies in the plethora of special interest groups spawned in an open society, some of them extraordinarily well funded. Special interests not only contribute to political corruption, but in the case of the most militant, terrorize politicians by threatening to concentrate upon their defeat unless their support is forthcoming on the issue deemed critical. It can be argued, of course, that such groups balance each other out, but that is not always the case. Clearly, certain interest groups have a degree of power, irrespective of whether their views accord with those of a majority of the citizenry, that is threatening to those in public office.

The enormous cost of "free elections" in our electronic society enhances the power of those with ample money, since the individuals running for office must have access to such funds. Professionals can now tell the aspiring politician approximately how much money he or she will need to win various offices, and what amount will guarantee a loss.

If the Western democracies, and especially the United States, have pioneered in these problems, they no longer stand apart from democracies in the non-Western world. The current trends in Japan, while still comparatively recent, run in the same direction. In South Korea and Taiwan also, similar issues are rising to the fore. In addition, there is the simple but basic matter of law and order. In a number of the new as well as the old democracies, the breakdown of social order and increasing crime are causing citizens to focus on security in the most immediate sense, namely, as it pertains to their homes and families.

As a result of these and related matters, one question now looms up with greater saliency than at any time in history: are modern pluralist societies governable? In this connection, the importance of leadership has once again been pushed to the front. The thesis, so popular at the turn of the century, that charismatic leadership would cease to be important, being succeeded by a new faceless, technocratic bureaucratic rule, must be discarded. If not charismatic, a leadership capable of communicating effectively with the people has never been more important. Perhaps the two most critical requirements for the open society are these: intellectuals and policy-makers who can live with complexity; and leaders who can translate that complexity into terms understandable to the citizenry without undue distortion.

To be successful, moreover, democratic leaders must have the capacity to mobilize their people on behalf of the policies deemed essential, and as close to the optimal time for their success as possible. Given the extraordinary pace with which events move in the current world and the proclivity in a democracy to shun sacrifices for the future in favor of immediate gratification, this requirement is extremely difficult to achieve.

Thus, when we survey the broad trends in Asia and elsewhere, we can note that the developmental tides sweeping over much of the world are pushing virtually every society in the direction of greater pluralism and more accessibility, and in many cases, interdependence, especially in the economic realm. We are entering the age of the borderless economy, and at a breathless pace. Economic activities on the part of the private sectors of the market economies are crossing political boundaries at will, and voluntarily or involuntarily, governments have relinquished some of their power to control such activities. It is for this among other reasons that many observers speak of the growing weakness of the state. Within bounds, the weakness of the state enables the greater freedom of the society. But the bounds are critical, because freedom can lead to license and anarchy, real or threatened, followed by a restoration of state power by force.

Indeed, in such diverse societies as the Soviet Union, China, South Korea, and Taiwan, we have witnessed a pendulum-like swing in the direction of liberty, then after its perceived excesses, in the direction of control. Of course, the degree of control exercised and the methods used have differed, but the swings have been similar. From these developments, a generalization can be drawn. Those who expect a lineal progression from less to greater political openness, from authoritarianism to democracy, are doomed to disappointment. In Asia and elsewhere, the excesses of one course will create an adverse response resulting in "corrections" until the excesses of the reverse course manifest themselves sufficiently to induce another shift. The intensity of the corrections, and their duration will depend upon many variables, domestic and external.

At the same time, a very important second fact should be noted. The extremities of the political continuum are in the course of being eliminated. On the one end, the traditional monarchies are disappearing from the scene: witness events in Nepal and even Bhutan. Irrespective of the course of the Gulf War, Saudi Arabia is next, as are the Emirates. Soon all variants of the pre-modern political order will be found only in history books. At the other end, the hard authoritarian systems of the 20th century are also on their way out. These have been systems that rested upon a huge concentration of power—military, economic, and political—in the hands of a small elite, ultimately a single individual, via refined organizational and indoctrinational techniques and a capacity to enforce a high degree of isolation, Instead, we shall witness a shorter continuum, ranging from soft authoritarianism to political openness, both being present in a variety of forms.

One advantage of this shorter continuum will be a greater capacity to communicate economically and culturally across political boundaries as, indeed, is already apparent. With that advantage comes a challenge, possibly a threat. The nation-state—so long the repository of ultimate power and loyalty for some, more recently so for many—can no longer exercise its sovereignty in the historic fashion to which citizens have become accustomed. Decision-making, hence, power, must be spread both downward and upward from the nation-state. The problems of the community can no longer be handled in the same degree from the center. And the need for decision-making structures above the nation-state is now increasingly accepted despite the enormous difficulties in establishing such structures so that they operate effectively.

Yet the nation-state will still be necessary, and indeed, for some time, it will remain the principal source of legitimacy for most citizens as well as the principal repository of power. Moreover, certain leaders and elites can be expected to fight vigorously to maintain the sovereignty of their nation. Indeed, the titanic struggle between nationalism and internationalism will be one of the great dramas of the coming decades, with fateful consequences for all inhabitants of the planet Earth.

In this context, democracy will play a complex role. The appeal to patriotism will strike a natural chord, and often, rightly or wrongly, it will continue to be the primary means of mobilization. Yet all nations, led by the major powers, will be forced by circumstances to move from unilateralism to multilateralism in matters of both foreign and domestic policy, and to accommodate to the rapidly advancing elements of cosmopolitanism in the economic and cultural spheres.

Meanwhile, economic development and accompanying social advances will guarantee greater political pluralism, hence, greater openness or freedom. In this sense, despite the retreats or retrenchments, democracy will advance in the long run in an even greater number of societies. But in the course of this trend, the state must not be overly weakened lest the authoritarian fall-back be severe. And one must neither expect nor want a total convergence of political systems given the major cultural, developmental, and spatial differences among societies.

When one surveys the new era and the challenges that accompany it, one can easily predict that the decades immediately ahead will constitute the most memorable years in the history of mankind. Science and technology will continue their advances, giving mankind an ever wider range of opportunities for material prosperity and cultural growth. It is the human element in the equation that is uncertain. Can we count on curbing the propensity of those with power for irrational or evil actions while still providing societies with a political system sufficiently coherent and strong to accomplish the complex tasks of modern governance? And can we count on the average citizens, given greater rights of political participation, to exercise the combination of judgment, tolerance, and restraint that alone will allow an open society to function? These are the central challenges faced by democracy—in Asia and elsewhere.

AMERICAN SECURITY IN THE ASIA-PACIFIC

Paul H. Kreisberg

Mr. Paul H. Kreisberg is a senior associate at the Carnegie Endowment for International Peace, working in the field of American policy in Asia. He holds a B.S.S. from City College, New York, and an M.A. from Columbia University. A former foreign service officer, he has also been director of studies at the Council on Foreign Relations, New York. He is a frequent contributor to various journals.

The United States has had two sets of overlapping strategies over the last 90 years for dealing with what is now called the Asia-Pacific region. Now it needs to develop a third, but is confronted with a global environment in which clarity and precision about strategy in any region of the world is extraordinarily difficult.

From 1900 to 1940 we saw the Pacific region as an isolated area of our security interests. We wanted an open door for American business: to prevent any other power—particularly Japan—from gaining an exclusive power base in the region and to assure that the United States was the paramount naval power in the region, capable of ensuring US safety behind the vast glacis of the Pacific Ocean. There was no particular concern about the economic or political development of the countries of the region nor about the welfare of their peoples. The colonial powers of Europe were still in control of most of the region outside China and Japan but, for the most part, US thinking about the Asia-Pacific was not directly linked with US security concerns about Europe or other regions. The decade between 1935–45 increasingly focused American attention on the threat from Japan as part of a global Axis attack on the West. This global perspective continued after the war, centered on the Soviet Union with its presumed powerful Asian regional surrogates in China, North Korea, and, as the 1950s developed, North Vietnam.

Post-war decolonization created more than a dozen independent but weak regional states vulnerable to direct or indirect communist threats and thus of importance to US military, political, and economic security interests. The United States supported all noncommunist governments, giving preference to those which were friendly or allied but aiding even those—like India or Indonesia—which preferred "non-alignment." None, except for Japan, was of major direct importance to US security. The "loss" of any one, however, threatened to undercut American power, influence, and credibility anywhere in the world; risked giving adversaries a strategic foothold athwart US lines of political or military communication in the Pacific and Indian Oceans; and potentially represented threats to other regional states.

Bilateral and multilateral alliances at times linked Asia, Europe, and North America. Although the multilateral ones gradually withered away, a system of base structures from Japan and South Korea through the Philippines, South Vietnam, Thailand, Australia, and Pakistan provided strategic and regional support for US forces throughout Asia and elsewhere in the world. The United States stood prepared to defend anyone threatened by a communist power, fought two major regional land wars, and stood to arms at sea on numerous other occasions to make this clear.

American trade and investment also flourished within this strategy although economic objectives, despite suspicions in some Asian countries, were never high on the US agenda. The economies of US friends and allies, particularly those in Northeast Asia and, somewhat more slowly, those in Southeast Asia flowered.

Japan, South Korea, Taiwan, the Philippines, Thailand, India, Pakistan, Indonesia, Singapore, Malaysia, South Vietnam (the central failure), Australia, New Zealand, and ultimately even China all, at various times, accepted the security benefits, and occasionally the obligations, of US strategy. The United States provided arms, military training, intelligence, occasionally became deeply involved in their defense through clandestine operations, provided huge volumes of bilateral economic and technical assistance, and facilitated access to international financial institutions for credits and loans.

In exchange, many countries backed US global policy interests at critical times, helped on sensitive security problems (particularly when both their own and US interests ran parallel), and enthusiastically sent hundreds of thousands of students to the United States for training and education. English increasingly became the *lingua franca* for educated Asians, particularly in business, economics, and science; the dollar became—as everywhere—the currency of preferred international use; and American popular culture—and values—spread widely throughout the region. American influence became paramount.

The security environment began to change in the broadest sense in the 1970s. The leadership of first China, then the USSR changed as did their national strategic policies. Both the global and regional threats from communist states declined.

- Soviet and Vietnamese troops were, for all practical purposes, out of Afghanistan, Cambodia, Vietnam, and Mongolia.

- Chinese and Soviet support for communist insurgencies stopped (the Khmer Rouge is a special case).

- North Korea came under pressure from China and the USSR to reduce tensions on the Korean peninsula and, pressed by strong domestic economic compulsions, is apparently responding, though slowly and reluctantly.

- All Asian communist states, except North Korea, reduced the size of their armed forces and lowered levels of military confrontation with their neighbors.

- China and the USSR normalized or dramatically improved relations with all Asian states from Indonesia and Singapore to South Korea and Japan.

- Vietnam's relations with all its ASEAN neighbors eased.

- Tensions across the Taiwan strait declined, even if the key political issues of reunification remained unresolved.

- Disputed islands in the South China Sea remained a potential source of conflict but first Beijing and, more recently, Jakarta suggested ways of easing tensions.

Identifying the threat to the United States became increasingly difficult. At the same time, the Vietnamese war and mounting US trade and budget deficits in the 1980s diminished US ability and willingness to "bear any burden" and certainly to "pay any cost." US technological and manufacturing advantages ebbed in the direction of more cost-efficient Asian economies.

The United States now found Japan its major economic competitor and American dependence on Japan and several other developing Asian economies, both for capital and key manufacturing imports, grew uncomfortably large. US aid to

Asia dimished sharply and US importance as a trading partner for Asian countries, while still high in 1991, was gradually shrinking. American insistence on "leveling" economic playing fields in Asia, gaining greater access to Asian markets, and reducing Asian trade surpluses intensified and, as a result, a host of trade, investment, and intellectual property disputes proliferated. These disputes began to sour bilateral relations and to brew new forms of anti-US sentiment in the region.

Political systems in Asia became more democratic and more pluralistic and less willing to accept authoritarian policy direction. Nationalistic pressures increased for greater "independence" from US influence. Resistance to US military presence on their territory, and unwillingness to accept US competition in long-protected domestic markets mounted. New generations of Asians grew to adulthood and positions of greater influence in their countries with scant memory of the post-war years in which US support for their new, weak, and impoverished governments was vital, or of the war years when Japan was an occupying power.

US political impatience with these changes and the declining security threat have brought increasing popular pressures for greater "burden sharing" by prosperous Asians:

- for Asian economic assistance to US strategic partners or friends elsewhere in the world;

- for more money to cover the costs of US forces in Asia, and lower compensation by the United States for base rights; and

- for greater sharing by Asian countries, particularly Japan, of the costs of a wide variety of US regional and global responsibilities—economic, ecological, social, and humanitarian, as well as security.

In some instances, with less intimate security "partners" and in cases where the United States has been quiet and subtle in its tactics, the response of Asians has been positive—Singapore's agreement to new air and naval access for the United States, hints from Brunei and Malaysia of similar willingness to be more cooperative, and Indian overflight and refueling facilities, frequent ship visit access, and much more active military to military interchange. With major partners, particularly Japan and the Philippines, where domestic political pressures on all sides were engaged, the problems have been more serious.

Who indeed are the enemies which US forces are defending against in Asia? Are they American enemies? Even if Soviet attack and missile submarines continued to sit in the Sea of Okhotsk, if "warning time" for war in Europe was stretching out to 1-2 years, what level of ready forces does the United States need to keep forward to deal with that threat in the Pacific? And if there are threats in other areas, such as the Middle East, Asians ask, is this really a concern of Asia-Pacific states? Asians still want some US "presence," almost exclusively for psychological reassurance except in Korea, but how much, and for what purposes no one is prepared to say and probably no one really knows. There are two major variables in all this: First, will US-Chinese and US-Soviet strategic and political relationships change? And, second, does the "new global order" presumably being set in place in the Persian Gulf change US security requirements?

Soviet and Chinese Policy

Conceivably, a hard-line military-influenced leadership could return to power in Moscow determined to restore domestic order, restore the unity of the USSR, and revive the eroding global perception of Soviet influence on world events. A similar power group could come to dominate policies in Beijing after Deng Xiaoping's death. Nevertheless, for the next decade and more both countries will be consumed by enormous and perhaps intractable domestic challenges. The Warsaw Pact and COMECON have collapsed as instruments of Soviet strategic policy. Neither communist "power" has the economic strength to provide help to other countries. "Communism" or even "socialism" does not offer an attractive model for social or economic development anywhere.

China and the Soviet Union could disrupt and complicate international order by supplying arms or other support to domestic dissidents around the world but, regardless of leadership changes at the top, strong political and economic opposition will argue against risking or supporting military ventures outside their borders. Soviet military adventurism, a Sino-Soviet conflict, military tension between Japan and the Soviets, or another "Afghanistan" all seem remote. Suspicion of China remains strong in Asia, a two-thousand year legacy, but has softened in response to Chinese policy in the last few years and is a long-term, not an immediate concern despite occasional murmuring to the contrary, particularly on Taiwan.

China and Taiwan

It is worth briefly recalling the statement of "US Policy" in sections 2 and 3 of the 1978 Taiwan Relations Act (TRA):

> 2(b)(4). Any effort to determine the future of Taiwan other than peaceful means, including by boycotts or embargos, are a threat to the peace and security of the Western Pacific area and of grave concern to the U.S. . . .

> 2(b)(6). It is U.S. policy to maintain the capacity of the U.S. to resist any resort to force or other forms of coercion that would jeopardize the security, or the social or economic system, of the people on Taiwan.

> 3(c). . . . . The President and the Congress shall determine, in accordance with constitutional processes, appropriate action by the U.S. in response to any such danger.

The United States continues to have wide leeway under this language and probably few in Congress or among the American public think much about the open-ended commitment to Taiwan. But neither is there any evidence that Beijing contemplates the use of force in the foreseeable future, despite occasional rash political bombast, although political tensions will rise if pro-independence influences grow in Taiwan in the next decade.

Chinese moves of the type envisaged in the TRA would pose a grave threat not just to US relations with China but could also fundamentally reverse the reality and the perception throughout Asia that China is not a threat, altering the entire character of Chinese relations with all its neighbors. There seems no reason to structure US forces or a US security policy for the region to give this contingency high priority, at least for the present. Like war with the Soviet Union, a potential war with China assumes a totally different global US policy, force structure, and political and economic relationships in Asia.

The Gulf War

This is a major variable for US security and the ultimate implications are beyond the scope of this paper. In February 1991, a number of adverse scenarios—an escalation of civilian casualties or material damage; the use of Chemical Weapons or Biological Weapons; an increase in discussion of the use of nuclear weapons (even if their use is not intended); rejection of "peace initiatives" which gather significant international support; the legislative defeat of new Japanese proposals for support for the United States, among numerous others—could severely damage US relations with Japan in fundamental political and security ways. There is widespread recognition within the US government, certainly at professional and mid-levels, that the danger of this increases the longer the war goes on. Current or prospective access to facilities or services throughout Asia could come under strong political and potentially violent opposition. Alternatively, a relatively quick and decisive resolution ending in Iraqi withdrawal and a major weakening of Iraq's military power would bolster respect for US military power and will, and strengthen US credibility throughout Asia.

Threats

Leaving these variables aside, what are the key security threat areas of concern to the United States in the region?

The Korean Peninsula

Nuclear proliferation in North Korea is one major security threat shared by Moscow, Beijing, and Tokyo, as well as Seoul. If the North is successful, South Korea will inevitably contemplate following suit. A storm of debate will burst over Japan with the question whether it, too, should consider a national nuclear deterrent and thus fundamentally rethink its security policies.

It is hard to see the counter-arguments for a policy package which included withdrawal of any US nuclear weapons still in the South, strong and internationally observable assurances from both Koreas to refrain from nuclear weapons development, trilateral guarantees of such assurances, and further guarantees that none of the nuclear powers will use nuclear weapons on the peninsula.

Reduction of military forces by both Koreas and strong confidence-building measures are also in US interests and those of all the regional powers. From a strictly US viewpoint, however, Korean détente and certainly anything approaching "unification" will obviate any prospects for South Korean participation in hypothetical regional "peace keeping" activities; accelerate the pace of US force withdrawal, which will eventually be total, from Korea; diminish or even eliminate the prospect of using facilities in South Korea for future regional contingencies; and ultimately assume a possible termination of the treaties either Korea has with other countries.

The Japanese are privately unenthusiastic about reunification and the South Koreans know this. The Chinese are probably equally unenthusiastic although they are less open about it. Who knows what the implications may be of a 75 million-person, energetic, and aggressive (in both the good and bad sense), industrial/raw material-rich power as a neighbor? From a US and Soviet viewpoint, a new "balancing" state in Northeast Asia looks more positive, so long as both countries maintain good relations with it and it is not a nuclear power.

Closer South Korean, Chinese, and Soviet relations provide a firebreak against new risks of North-South conflict. All these parties and the Japanese talk to one another regularly about security on the peninsula. And consideration among these of bringing North Korea into the net in an informal "six party" dialogue on security in the general Korean peninsula area may make a further contribution to this process.

Japan

No review of potential "threats" would be complete without a reference to Japan as an incipient security concern, a concern that lurks in the back of everyone's mind—Chinese, Soviet, the rest of Asia, the United States. Japan exerts little direct impact on political and security questions in the Asia-Pacific, but economic influence indirectly carries with it tacit political weight. Japan's huge industrial mobilization base, technological capabilities, financial strength, and economic leverage could make it, in a relatively brief period, a major global military and political power and, in combination with another major power other than the United States, capable of transforming global power relationships.

Continued close relations between Japan and the United States, Japanese engagement in any and all regional cooperative organizations, close economic and political relations by all the Asian states with Japan, continued minimalization of Japanese military forces in Asia, and limited further growth in Japanese defense forces are widely seen in Asia as critical policies to avert these potential contingencies.

Other Threats

American and Asian specialists and, occasionally, high officials have pointed out other potential security threats in the region but there is *no* justification for any US commitment to become militarily involved in any of these. For example:

- Another regional war on the subcontinent cannot be excluded but is unlikely to spread farther, although all the major powers share a common interest in making diplomatic efforts to avert such a war and particularly the use of nuclear weapons. Some in the United States and Asia argue that, in theory, Indian military ground, naval, and air power could be turned against Southeast Asia or be used to interdict the SLOCs. This is, frankly, a fairy tale scenario.

- Burma is tense with internal unrest and China is currently fueling Burmese government military capabilities with large quantities of conventional weapons. Weapons are already "filtering" into India, Bangladesh, and Thailand from Burma but there is no reason for US involvement.

- In theory, Malay and ethnic Chinese tensions in Southeast Asia could spill over into heightened national rivalries, or Vietnamese ambitions over the last forty years for Indochinese hegemony could revive—but these are dim, dim prospects. All parties in the region are attentive to finding cooperative political, and in some cases military ways of minimizing the risks.

Intra-ASEAN military cooperation has been quietly growing though there is still great hesitancy about formalizing security arrangements. Quiet encouragement of continuing expansion of military contingency planning and coordination within ASEAN is clearly in US interests as is the continuation of US military training programs, encouragement of greater interoperability among ASEAN military forces through military sales, and formal and informal engagement in exercises with ASEAN military, both individually or in groups. Closer consultation, exchanges, and cooperation at military and civilian levels between ASEAN countries and India and continuation of this same trend between Australia and India and the United States and India are also important in gradually building mutual confidence among countries in the region, enhancing perceptions of mutual interest in regional security, and avoiding conflict.

The United States will remain the strongest military power in Asia but, as noted earlier, the resources and political support—at home or abroad—to sustain unilateral or even effective bilateral policies in the absence of sharply definable threats is uncertain. Linking US security concerns with those of multiple partners, and through these with the larger international community, is both an economic necessity and a political virtue. That is what is being done in the Persian Gulf, with the largest share of financial costs and a considerable portion of ground and air combat burden being borne by regional states and other western partners.

The "new international order" cannot in the future mean *unilateral* US defense in Asia of any country or government under threat. Of course, this was not US policy in the past *except* when communist challenges were involved. US military forces were not a factor in any of the key non-communist related regional crises in Asia over the last four decades, except for the surprise (to the Navy) ordering of the *Enterprise* to the Indian Ocean in 1971. They have "shown the flag"on numerous less dramatic occasions, in humanitarian circumstances, in connection with piracy, and during joint exercises. It is the communist threat that now seems to be declining.

Alternative Strategies

Under these circumstances there appear to be three alternative approaches to security policy:

1. *Continued maintenance of unilateral US capabilities to act to defend countries of our choice or with whom we have specific defense alliances even when threats come from other than communist countries.* There is no sign of any consensus or even interest in the United States in such a strategy.

2. *Organization of some regional "constabulary" force or informal understandings on pooling forces to join with the United States to deal with potential contingencies.* At some point far down the future track, when confidence and political and military relationships among countries of Asia develop sufficiently, this might be conceivable. Tentative efforts could be possible even earlier if missions were limited in very narrow terms involving very low levels of force and were not directed against any sovereign power—but to an anti-piracy, anti-smuggling, an international "coast guard" service, for example.

Including Japan, China, Vietnam, or the Soviet Union in anything larger is probably not politically practicable or even wise at this time. ASEAN members should be encouraged to work out arrangements for security cooperation among themselves before attempting to engage in a larger regional security enterprise whose responsibilities would be difficult to define, more difficult to administer, and whose overt leadership by the United States would raise problems everywhere.

3. *Maintaining a minimum strategic force capability to balance continuing Soviet strategic forces in the Far East until these are further diminished unilaterally or by mutual agreement.* But at the same time the United States should actively encourage regional and subregional discussions, and institutions, to build stability with assurances and guarantees from all the major military powers.

Forward-based US forces would gradually be reduced as would active US base facilities. When needed and in accordance with regional consensus on their need, and with international support outside the region. US forces would be surged to facilities maintained by states within the region: The Persian Gulf model. Strategic reserves of supplies would be maintained at selected areas within the region including in the Philippines, Japan, Australia, Singapore, and perhaps one or more other sites if agreement could be reached on such arrangements. US ships and aircraft would regularly, but in small units, deploy throughout the region for small-scale exercises, good-will and other visits, but much less frequently with larger size ships.

There are five central premises for this latter strategy other than a continued low threat environment throughout the region from *major* threats:

1. *Japan.* The US-Japan security treaty must remain in effect and Japan must accept greater international peacekeeping responsibilities within the context of UN decisions. The first is critical to ensuring confidence within the region about Japanese policies. The second is vital for any possible Japanese concurrence as well as to ensure consensus in the United States for continuing security cooperation with Japan.

Japan has moved carefully but clearly toward more support for international security efforts—civilian UN observer missions, contributions to UN peacekeeping, plans for larger engagement in UN efforts in Cambodia—until the Gulf war complicated the political environment in Japan. Fifty years after World War II Japan must come to grips with its international political responsibilities and these must be recognized by other Asian states.

Japan should, however, continue to disavow the use of force within the Asia-Pacific region, other than in self-defense, unless there is strong support within the region to the contrary. Japan does not need a significantly larger military capability than it has at present so long as the Japan-US security treaty remains in effect and threats remain low in the region. US air, marine, and naval forces based in Japan should gradually be reduced, with the pace geared both to Japanese-Soviet relations and North-South Korean tensions. Japanese base facilities should be kept available for US use in major international security contingencies.

A fundamental premise of this policy is increasingly active engagement of Japan in discussions and policy coordination with the US on international security issues as they evolve and as policies are formulated on both sides.

2. *China* must be encouraged to play a role in regional economic and political forums. This latter view is widely accepted in Asia but Sino-US tensions over domestic Chinese policies threaten to flare repeatedly in coming years and undercut regional cooperation and consensus. However Americans, individually or even through official statements, may choose to reflect moral indignation about developments in China, US strategy requires that it cooperate with China toward its being at least a benign and at best an actively helpful partner in preserving stability from Korea through the Taiwan Straits to Southeast Asia and the Himalayas.

3. *Regionally,* smaller countries must gradually accept greater collective responsibility for security in their own areas of Asia, particularly ASEAN in Southeast Asia and, a more distant hope. South Asian Association for Regional Cooperation (SAARC) member cooperation in the Indian Ocean. Weapons of mass destruction must be limited, regional states should consult or at least keep their neighbors informed when they are designing force levels and considering weapons procurement in order to avoid increasing bilateral tensions. Consultations on political, economic, and security issues at a variety of levels should be expanded. The United States should offer to participate in any of these where its presence might be welcome.

4. *Security treaties* or agreements will continue to be important and should not be easily abandoned or altered, particularly those with Japan and Australia. The frequency with which the United States conducts *large* exercises should be carefully restrained so long as the general threat environment remains low. But in that environment the possibility for continuing expansion of smaller exercises with regional states may increase and *no* states with which the United States has

friendly relations should be excluded, including communist states.

5. *Economically,* growth and rising standards of living have become increasingly significant in contributing to a sense of national security. Japan. South Korea, Taiwan, China, and several other Asian states provide economic or technical assistance to other Asians states and elsewhere as well. The United States has virtually opted out of this sector in the Asia-Pacific, except for diminishing aid for the Philippines and Indonesia.

Domestic US economic and social policy is outside the specific terms of reference of this paper. But the United States cannot have a credible and successful security policy in the Asia-Pacific region if it is not strong at home. Domestic weakness and division invariably translates into perceptions of international weakness, bilateral and multilateral economic friction, and a weakening of US political influence regardless of how strong our nominal defenses may seem.

Regional Cooperation

Recognition of the importance of greater regional consultation and cooperation in the Asia-Pacific has grown during the last decade, but there are widely differing views on what should be discussed and through what kinds of forums—particularly as private groups or semi-official groups have given way to governmental groups.

- Some are wary that ASEAN could be weakened by the Asia-Pacific Economic Cooperation ministerial-level meetings which began in 1989.

- Initial preference for cooperation among "like-minded" states—democracies, market economies—is wisely shifting to a more "inclusive" concept embracing China and, potentially, all Asia-Pacific states from Vietnam to the USSR.

- Some advocate an exclusive Asian economic group to protect "Asian" interests which would exclude North America, Australia, and New Zealand. This idea is unlikely to flourish unless there is a fundamental breakdown of the current global economic trading and financial system, but it does have the potential to seriously weaken prospects for future US political and security cooperation with Asian states.

- Others, thus far with little Asian support, argue for a broad Asian forum which would explicitly address a broad range of political and security issues, including human rights and social issues, as well as economic ones.

- The Soviets have suggested a variety of regional and subregional forums focused on everything from security to economic cooperation, primarily as a way of engaging Moscow more deeply in Asia-Pacific issues. They have gotten little support thus far. Nevertheless a subregional conference (USSR, United States, China, both Koreas, Japan) designed to provide guarantees for Northeast Asian security has been welcomed, in principle, by South Korea and Beijing and may be helpful should North-South Korean discussions progress and Soviet-Japanese relations continue to improve.

Institutional structure is less important than increasing regularization of meetings among senior ministers and other officials (this is a central stumbling point for China in finding a formula under which it would be willing to sit with Taiwan). Inevitably at such gatherings an increasingly broad range of issues will arise, including security and political concerns, either around the table or in corridors, regardless of the formal agenda. Greater security does not come simply from the process of such meetings or conversations but through contacts and mutual familiarization with one anothers' views and concerns. In the opening of options for new meetings and interaction in sub-regional groupings tensions are likely to be eased. The process does not replace the need for military security measures but, over time, it is indispensible for "confidence-building."

The question of who should be included in any gathering of Asian-Pacific states is more complex. East and Southeast Asians generally agree on one another as the core as well as Australia, New Zealand, the United States, and some representation for the South Pacific islands. Taiwan and Hong Kong, as well as China and, eventually, Vietnam. North Korea, and

Burma come next. There is much less consensus on the Soviet Union but eventually Soviet participation (or whoever may appropriately represent Moscow in such forums) is necessary. There is no thought of including South Asia. Nor have the South Asian states given much thought to how they should or could engage themselves with East and Southeast Asia.

Direct military issues will not be on the early agenda of any of these meetings but they will contribute to security nevertheless. US and Asian senior civilian and military authorities meet regularly in a variety of ways and this should continue, and increase. Senior military commanders who never used to see each other—US, Indian, Japanese, South Korean, and ASEAN—now meet to "play golf", and this contact is being extended to include limited or quasi-military exercises among various countries. Civilian defense authorities are ranging even more widely.

The Soviets and the United States exchanged ship visits in 1990. Some US officials doubt the wisdom of continuing this in the future but that is almost certainly a mistake. Even the Japanese and Soviets are quietly exploring initial military-to-military exchanges, although at the level of senior officers, not military units. There is some Asian military interaction with China and this is likely to increase. Unfortunately, US contacts with the Chinese military remain frozen since Tienanmen but thought is being given to reviving Defense College exchanges and, at some point, further interaction may be helpful, although military sales may have to wait a long time.

The Fluid Situation

The summary thrust of this paper is that the security environment has changed, is continuing to change, and that being unequivocal about strategic options is impossible. The absence of clearly definable threats to the United States or to most individual Asian states makes a more cooperative, collaborative, inclusive approach to US security the most plausible one. The key countries, whose involvement and engagement are most critical to ensuring peace and stability in the region, as opposed to the larger global arena where the Soviet Union remains more important, are China and Japan. US military strategy can now draw forces from a variety of global theaters in a diminished global threat environment in order to deal with any potential regional threats. The primary US basing requirement is likely to be for clear but contingent access rather than for large in-being forces in the Asia-Pacific region. Finally, regionalization of discussions about Asian issues is growing and, although there are differences about structure and participation, these are likely over time to contribute to the easing of tensions and to enhancing stability and US security.

TECHNOLOGY
AND MILITARY ORGANIZATION
IN ASIA

Dr. Paul Bracken

Dr. Paul Bracken holds B.S. and M.S. degrees from Columbia University and a Ph.D. from Yale University where he presently teaches. He has also been associated with the Hudson Institute, Ketron, Inc., and the Fels Center of Government, the University of Pennsylvania. Dr. Bracken is the director of Yale International Security Programs and coordinator of International Management Studies at the Yale School of Management. He is the author of **Burden of Victory,** editor of **Changing Dimensions of Security in Asia,** and co-editor of **The New Security System in Europe.**

This paper looks at the problems associated with the proliferation of advanced military technology in Asia from an institutional rather than exclusively a weapons framework. Instead of categorizing the problem into types of weapon proliferation (nuclear, chemical, biological, ballistic missile, and other advanced conventional weapons) and describing relevant incentives and controls, an institutional analysis is suggested which focuses on how importing or developing these technologies could affect civil-military relations, macro-organizational behavior, and internal (as distinct from external) norms against proliferation.

In many cases, the military, who hold positions of power in Asia, are the decision makers. Even when it is *not* the military, the military will almost always be important players in proliferation decisions and their consequences. For example, there will be pressure to integrate the chosen items into military units (they are, after all, weapons); to protect them; to produce operationally useful numbers of them; and to ensure reliable supplies needed to maintain them. The military also can play a negative role, for example, in a leadership's desire to keep possession of advanced weapons by relying on special guards who do not report to the military. Still, military organizations are critical actors in the process.

The existing research on non-proliferation serves a useful purpose and no criticism of it is intended by this different approach. Traditional approaches focus on external norms and restraints—those supplied by other states or the international system to check or slow the spread of these technologies. With an emphasis on safeguards, the NPT, fuel assurances, and inspection systems, control is supplied from outside the state. The opprobrium incurred by openly crossing one of the major proliferation thresholds is itself an external norm, and is one of the main anti-proliferation tools. Looking only at external norms and restraints is insufficient, however, for two reasons.

First, the decision to acquire these technologies is a political one in that it is a collective choice by a group of people. The central phenomena of proliferation revolve around military and political organizations—the institutional approach. While it is possible that this group decision will be made after carefully weighing the costs and benefits of alternative defense policies, experience suggests that norm-based behavior, rather than calculation, will be an important factor in deciding what to do. The norms that will bear on the decision may be cultural, organizational, or political—but they will certainly be weighted toward internal rather than external norms supplied by an international, mainly Euro-American, system of states.

A second reason for taking an institutional approach is that importing or developing advanced military technology can have major unintended effects in addition to its direct impact on the regional military balance. Pakistani and Indian nuclear weapon programs may lead to military instability of a kind feared in the Soviet-American arms competition, as a reciprocal fear of surprise attack leads to a dreaded escalation spiral. But it may also produce fundamental changes in the civil-military relations of each state. Development of a nuclear bomb is an extraordinary managerial achievement involving coordination of many different technical, personnel, and financial facets. Managing such a large effort demonstrates, and creates, administrative competence. If it is undertaken by the military, their status and competence increase. Both of these, status and competence, can be directed to other objectives, and the overall capacity of the military organization increases while that of other institutions declines in a relative sense.

Non-military institutions will often not possess the tight discipline and organization of the military. Civil institutions in developing countries frequently are no more than arenas for interest group politics. As such, they have great difficulty serving as vehicles for modernization. But the military, with their discipline and organization, can break through the paralyzing effects of interest group politics. In many situations development of complex military systems will necessitate breaking through comparable political barriers. So the successful adoption of advanced military technologies can lead to an increased general capacity for state building, strengthening the military institution inside government. The ensuing results are case-dependent, but can include subduing regional or ethnic sub-groups, eliminating enemies of the leadership, and increasing the efficiency of extractive mechanisms to pay for it all. This was, after all, how most states came to be states in the first place. There are clear signs that the same process is at work in the developing world, with country specific variations.

Depending on the extent to which advanced technology is actually integrated into military organizations—as distinct from merely acquiring prototype units—changes in state structure can be far reaching. New organizations of unusually high reliability are needed, and new status, roles, and power can transform military and government organizations. In the superpowers, nuclear weapons led to the creation of an entire new set of state and military organizations: SAC, the SRF (the Soviet strategic rocket forces), North American Air Defense, Central Intelligence Agency and KGB—the Committee of State Security, the Russian Secret Police—intelligence centers reporting directly to political leaders and bypassing military channels, the NSC and the Defense Council in the Politburo all either grew directly out of the nuclear era, or were dramatically changed by it.[1] In addition, major weapon laboratories, links with universities, interest groups, and influential think tanks resulted from the acquisition of these technologies by the first nuclear powers. Some of these organizations might have been created had nuclear weapons never been invented, but they would not have the character that they developed with nuclear forces. The introduction of new technologies in Asia offers many contrasts to the superpower pattern, nonetheless, Asia is an especially interesting case because of the different political and military institutions and history there compared to those of the first four nuclear states, and to Western countries generally.

Military Institutions in Asia

The military institutions of Asia vary greatly from one state to the next; Japan is not like Indonesia, and South Korea is not like India. Asia has more heterogeneity among its military than any other region. What accounts for this, and why does it matter? The Asia-Pacific region is strategically and militarily disconnected. Intense repeated wars, such as occurred in

Europe, did not lead to a tightly coupled balance of power system. Asian military institutions have been driven as much by domestic factors as by the need to deal with external threats. In addition, the civilian control of the military that evolved in Europe, only reaching completion after World War II, did not develop the way it has in Asia. In Western Europe civilian control of the military is stable, and has become strongly institutionalized. Even where such control exists and has become a tradition in Asia, it is not clear that it is institutionalized. Things could change, upsetting the internal civil-military balance of power, as it already has in some countries. For all of these reasons what may be termed "the strategic cultures" of Asian states are very different from those we are used to in the West. This should be kept in mind when designing nonproliferation norms, since the institutional development in Asia is so different that Euro-American conceived external norms may be ineffective in the different strategic culture.

In Europe, military organizations converged structurally through fighting and learning from each other. For instance, the general staff system appeared first in Prussia, and its success in coordinating large bodies of men and integrating military and foreign policy led to it being copied by all the large powers of Europe (save Britain). Comparable integrating mechanisms in Asia have not developed. Even in militaristic states like North Korea, the general staff is thoroughly penetrated by the values of the party leadership and does not make independent assessments and judgments outside of narrowly constrained boundaries. In India, an integrated general staff system with a senior commander does not even exist, and is extremely controversial politically. Senior military staffs in Asia do not only plan international strategy; they administer political guidance, they play in domestic politics, and they even make (some) economic decisions. Many of them are highly professional, but they are professional in a very different way than what we have come to know through a Eurocentric perspective.

Development Paths As another example of the different development path in Asia compared to Europe, in Europe the industrial revolution led to the harnessing of the national economy to military ends, so that an important part of every European military army was its support staff, those who integrated the domestic economy with the needs of the military. The availability of military technology today has changed so that Asian states can source from the larger world economy, rather than depending solely on domestic production.[2] Their supply lines are more global than anything seen in Europe—and this removes a considerable dependency of the military on the civilian economy.

In Europe, civilian control of the military grew out of this dependence. The military needed a technologically advanced national economy to expand and modernize because there were no other alternative sources for the needed weapons. But in Pakistan, Indonesia, the Philippines, and other countries advanced technology can be sourced from the world marketplace. The military can pay for its needs by gaining control of key commodity sectors, petroleum in Indonesia, or coconut oil in the Philippines (under Marcos), rather than having to run an entire economy. Historically, the military's inability to run the whole economy made it impossible for them to stay in power in Europe—they were compelled to turn over control to civilians who possessed far greater technical expertise and political legitimacy for this task. Clearly, a very different process is at work in much of Asia.

The American policy of containment allowed Asian military institutions to develop without much regard for the threat of external attack (save in the case of Korea), and this factor, too, insulates the military from many of the demands of national defense, allowing them to turn to domestic state building. Even in China, where there was a danger of external threat from the Soviet Union, it is remarkable how much domestic reasons influenced the development of Chinese military institutions rather than the task of defending national territory. The PLA was deeply involved with communist state making (a role not without real tensions). Then the Chinese military was suddenly called on to take seriously its national security role against the Soviet Union after being directed to other tasks during the cultural revolution. Because it had not been well prepared for many problems followed from this switch.

In the Far East there was nothing like NATO, a mechanism to standardize the military institutions into a common pattern. West European military organizations became even **more** similar after World War II than before because of NATO and the Warsaw Pact. Advanced technology accelerated this convergence, as national military organizations began to blend into a single organism. The addition of Airborne Early Warning and Control System, JSTARS, NATO Air Defense Ground Environment, and the NATO Planning Group, reshaped the command structure to become a truly integrated cross-border entity. The formation of NATO air into Allied Tactical Air Forces, and of its armies into echelons above corps further increased convergence. In the Warsaw Pact standardization was even greater, based, of course, on the Soviet model.

Across bloc lines there was a convergence of norms and expectations that grew directly out of the similarity in the forms of military organization between NATO and the Pact. Coalition membership created a common basis for the meaning of political and military signals, thresholds, a common interest in avoiding crises (nowadays referred to as confidence building), and subordination to superpower control. A decades-long process of organizational learning took place in which various crises tested and strengthened the stability of the system. There was nothing like this in Asia, and there *is* nothing like it in the country where it would today be of the greatest value—Korea. The greater variation of military institutions in Asia, relative to other regions, also means that when these institutions do confront one another there is a much slighter basis for shared understandings and concerns. The stark differences in the military organizations in China, India, Pakistan, the Soviet Union, and others are so great that it is hard to even conceive what a crisis management regime would look like.

Asia In Asia, military organization is shaped not only by a history radically different than Europe's, but by the fact that political institutions were recreated after World War II. Social revolutions transformed the political landscape, changing all of the state's institutions (including the military), altering class structures, and profoundly changing the ideological direction of most Asian societies. Such a transformation produces domestic tensions and problems and these, if they lead to unacceptable levels of disorder, invite military intervention into politics. One significant feature of many Asian military institutions is this potential threat to civilian governance.

In Pakistan and Indonesia the military already has a direct role in governance. In India the possibility is something which shapes a whole range of administrative relationships between the military and the state. India has not been subject to military rule since independence, but the examples of Pakistan, Indonesia, and others make this a potential that, in many respects, parallels the way that European militaries learned from each other in the 19th and early 20th century. Military rule is a model that can produce its own kind of learning in other states—something Samuel Finer refers to as the coup trap.[3]

In China and North Korea a potential for excessive military influence is also a potential that shapes administrative policy toward the military. At first glance, and based on a widely accepted theory of civil-military relations in communist states, the military is not and cannot be politicized to the point of threatening seizure of power from civilian Party leaders. The reason is that the Party thoroughly penetrates the high command, removing the distinction between party and military. Yet there are grounds for doubting the robustness of this theory, given what happened in Eastern Europe in 1989. While in no case did East European militaries enforce a Tiananmen Square solution on the threat posed to their rule, they also did nothing actively to prevent the fall of communist governments in East Germany, Czechoslovakia, or Hungary, even when overtures were made to them. In Poland they supported a coup which made the ultimate removal of communism inevitable, while in Rumania they openly turned against the leadership and its paramilitary arm. Each of these cases was special; Rumania and Hungary are hardly typical examples of communist civil-military relations. Yet these states are products of their history just as China and North Korea are of theirs, and it would be naive and, given the events of 1989, unwise to dismiss the possibility of some sort of military takeover or even civil war in Asia's remaining communist states.

North Korea North Korea is an especially interesting case because from the outside it seems so overwhelmingly focused on preparing for war against the South. But the organization of North Korea's armed forces is determined not only by capability against Seoul, but by the task of preventing potential centers of power from emerging to challenge the leadership. It is difficult enough to command a unified force with clear lines of authority; the North Korean command contains many diverse subparts requiring very high levels of coordination and control that are difficult to reconcile with military efficiency. An extraordinary matrix system of party and military control goes far beyond that in other communist states. Enormous effort is placed on standardizing political behavior within the military through the so-called "Army-Party Committees" which monitor and educate the troops to the Kim line.[4] The dual reporting channels within the military (whereby commanders answer to military superiors and party officials placed inside the organization) increases the organizational friction involved in getting anything done.

Another set of coordination costs arises from North Korea's bifurcated command system that results from Pyongyang's strategy of integrating ordinary military units with irregular ones. North Korea has the highest percentage of irregular warfare forces of any military organization in the world, with fully one-seventh of its army—24 brigades and some 100,000 soldiers—organized into special warfare, strategic reserve, and ranger units. North Korea also has a large terror, assassination, and infiltration force organized into many different units. How all of these work together is not known, but it appears that in many cases there are long vertical reporting chains tied to Kim Jong Il.

On paper, these diverse subparts of the North Korean military are neatly coordinated through reporting lines to the Ministry of the People's Armed Forces, Central Committee, and General Staff. This is hard to accept in practice. Operations of this diversity and complexity would require extensive lateral coordination of a kind that does not seem to exist, and moreover, runs contrary to the extreme top-down central control of the two Kims. It seems probable that various irregular warfare and special units are separated from the army in order to have a loyal organization that could counter potential army moves against the leadership. (This is not unlike the system employed by Nicolae Ceausescu in Rumania) and, it seems likely that the overall unified direction of the North Korean armed forces incurs substantial penalties as a consequence.

The information processing costs in this system must be enormous. By making coordination at any level below that of the top leadership difficult because of reliance on extreme compartmentation, a mixture of very different kinds of operations, and a political cross-checking of military decisions, the strategic apex is made more secure from internal disruption. Large, parallel security structures are coordinated only at the apex, and disloyalty not dealt with through the rigorous socialization of the North Korean officer corps is met by driving up the organizing costs for those who would work against the regime.

The problem is intrinsic to any state without institutionalized civilian control of the military, even if it is one of a degree short of what is conceivable in North Korea. India, Japan, the Philippines, South Korea, and China all face the problem of managing military structures which, if they grow too large and powerful, could exert undue influence on the state, even if an actual military takeover is a remote possibility. The politicization of the officer corps in Pakistan and Indonesia provides a model of what could happen, just as the Prussian general staff provided a model for 19th century European states. At the same time, for obvious strategic reasons, the problem cannot be dealt with by chopping the size of the military down to small manageable levels. These states face potential external dangers, or pressure from allies, and it would be reckless for them to disarm. Disarmament could also create new domestic vulnerabilities.

All Asian military institutions are shaped by twin forces: the external dangers and threats arising from the push and pull of international politics, and the domestic ordering of social and political forces. The real tension in Asia lies not between the civil and the military, but rather at the intersection of these two forces. International and domestic pressures can pull in different directions, upsetting old equilibriums and straining regional stability. In Asia tensions have been in good balance during the Cold War, but the likely downsizing of the US presence in the western Pacific will remake the international political system with unknown consequences for the future of Asian military institutions.

Technology and Military Organization

Despite the great variation apparent in Asia there are some common characteristics of military organization. Broadly speaking, most regional military organizations are large, undifferentiated infantry armies. Asia has seven of the ten largest armies in the world—a reflection of the population size of the region and the substitution of labor for military capital in organization. While the exceptions are obvious in Australia and Japan, for example, in China, India, Pakistan, Indonesia, and in Southeast Asia, armies are the most important part of the military. These armies mainly consist of large numbers of relatively poorly trained soldiers with little projection capability aside from that arising out of the pure mass of numbers. One of the most significant ways that advanced military technology could affect the Asian military, then, is by transforming the entire nature of these forces from mass infantry to modern military instruments. In theory, a little technology could go a long way. An army with modern air defense cover, or one with long-range striking capability could be far more effective than one without it.

US military policy has recognized the potential for military technology exports to create a high technology edge to otherwise low-tech forces. As advanced technology in general is a critical element in economic and defense power, one way of thinking about it is as a strategic currency, using exports to help countries who are friendly and isolating those who are not. There is no question that the security of Asia is affected by the American military technology advantage.[5] Our relationship with China has had this element. When there was concern about possible Soviet intimidation or even attack on China in the 1970s, the thrust of the US military response was to consider technology options for sending things like air defense radars, communications intelligence, and the like, providing China with hardware that it could not develop on its own. Our tie to South Korea clearly has a similar element in it, using technology to maintain a military balance on the peninsula.

There are several problems with using technology as the basis for US relationships, of course. Advanced technology is not always a usable currency in international relations because there are so many other important variables. For one thing the United States no longer has the monopoly that it once held in this area. At the very advanced end of the spectrum, where the United States still leads, it may be unwise to have so much specialization of the American economy, especially as the commercial technology base lags behind that of other states. Moreover, US technology relationships can themselves become embroiled in controversy. The controversy with Japan over the FSX fighter and the Toshiba export of machine tools to the Soviet Union demonstrate that even with a good ally relations can sour rather than improve. The effects of exporting military technology are more complex than merely winning friends and isolating potential foes. They can have significant, unrecognized effects on the receiving nation.

Technology can have a complex effect on the internal organization and distribution of power in states. No simple relationship exists between technology and changes in civil-military relations. It has been suggested that the increasing technological sophistication of a force would lead to greater autonomy of the military by creating more expertise that would clash with many of the political and administrative controls placed on military institutions.6 However, tests of this proposition have not supported such a simple relationship.7

Here we return to a basic distinction. There can be little doubt that early theories that a military could not be both expert (that is, professional) and controllable by political authorities misconstrued the civil-military relations problem. Too many examples exist of all sorts of expert professionals being easily controlled within a bureaucratic structure. Instead of focusing on the civil-military organizational seam, it is more instructive to examine the competing pressures between domestic socio-economic factors and international politics. Changes in either of these can have a profound effect on military organization. One general tendency has already been noted, the ability of many military organizations to source from a global rather than a purely domestic market. Changes in the resources available, the strategic environment, or the capacity of institutions can have important political and organizational consequences. As with any description of the Asian military, there are large differences in these pressures from one country to the next.

Consider the Indian armed forces. The Indian military has long considered itself an island of order that contrasts with the disorder in Indian society. Its major role has been to hold the state together by providing a cohesive institution that would back, but not threaten the state. This has been fundamental, and has been the strongest factor in its organizational history. But there is another obvious pressure from the push and pull of the regional system around India. In wars with China and Pakistan the army has been called to serve the external interests of the state. The adjustment between these two roles is what fundamentally shapes the Indian army.

The Indian military has so far been thoroughly subordinated to civilian control. One of the greatest concerns in India has been to maintain this relationship, and a major problem has been between balancing internal and external demands. In order to insure that military influence does not encroach on civilian power the post of military Commander-in-Chief was abolished at Independence. India does not have a general staff, but, instead, a loosely coordinated committee of service chiefs, the result of resistance to the creation, in the high command, of integrating mechanisms. Lateral relations among military units are relatively poorly developed at the large unit level, as are cross service coordination and planning. But this gap is hardly an accident. Full development of a lateral command system, such as a general staff system, and full inclusion of the military in foreign policy decisions would create a much stronger and more effective military institution. The benefits of this, given the Asian and Indian setting, could be considerable. Such a system could also strengthen the Indian military into what would be far and away the strongest institution in Indian society. Their values could encroach and displace those of the ruling establishment, and so there is considerable political and social pressure not to permit the full organizational development of the Indian high command.

Technology enters the picture because certain kinds of technology are only effective when placed in an appropriate command organization. Indeed, certain kinds of technology encourage organizational restructuring. Here it must be said that the type of technology matters. There is a large difference between mechanizing an army, that is, buying tanks and motorized fighting vehicles, and acquiring a nuclear weapon or a large national air defense system. New military technologies can be prototype units—where only one or a few systems are developed—or they can be mass-produced systems like tanks or other vehicles. Some military technologies expand the vertical information processing capacity of the organization: communications, command and control, and other systems, for example. Of these, some may involve a continuous output of information as with radars and some intelligence systems. The organizational effects will depend greatly on the kind of technology, and the way it is integrated into the organization.

The character of nuclear forces and ballistic missiles that go beyond prototype development to full deployment is to pressure for a thorough cross integration of warning and intelligence agencies, military formations, general staff planning roles, and industrial support. That, at least, has been the experience in other states who have acquired these weapons. The United States, Britain, France, and the Soviet Union all experienced major high command and force restructuring to absorb these new technologies. In the first three of these there has not been undue military influence, although in the Soviet Union there has been such a development, albeit slowly over many years. The important point is that socio-economic conditions of these states are very different from those existing in Asia.

The effects of adapting new military technology are complex and often unintended. They are not fully controllable. Scholarly studies of this phenomenon point to major unanticipated consequences, such as a need to overhaul a state's system for paying for the military, changes in professional identity, new arenas for opportunism, and a more disciplined and effective kind of state machinery.[8] In India, for example, deployment of a nuclear missile force would very likely entail a more thorough integration of the high command—integration of a kind that has, so far, been resisted by political leaders. It would also pressure India toward a changing ethnic composition of its army to administer the new force, and would likely involve the army more in international technology sourcing as a means to supply and maintain its new arm. One way around this, is to keep any new force small and tightly controlled, without integrating it wholesale into a restructured high command.

Pakistan is an even more vivid example of how changing domestic and international factors can produce changes in state and military organization. The war in Afghanistan led to a major expansion of the Pakistani Inter-Services Intelligence Directorate (ISI). ISI's resources increased greatly during the Afghan war through its distribution of American and Saudi arms and aid. Under Zia it became one of the most important and effective intelligence services in all Asia.[9] It has had a major role not only in managing the guerrilla war in Afghanistan but also in Kashmir and in internal Pakistani politics. Allegedly, it has also been crucial in securing critical components and technology for the Pakistani nuclear program as well. In contrast to the Indian nuclear program, the Pakistani nuclear program has far greater military input and supervision, and the mixing of a highly politicized intelligence agency with technology sourcing for the nuclear program is something that changes the fundamental character of Pakistani political institutions.

The preference for Pakistan's military to buy off-the-shelf arms has closely linked its local manufacturing to the world market. Pakistan Ordinance Factories (POF), a division of the Defense Ministry, has technology transfer agreements with China, Germany, Sweden, and the United States. It has concentrated the nation's largest pool of skilled industrial workers and technicians, some 40,000 employees in 14 factories. This has major implications for Pakistan's future development. Along with ISI and POF, there are other institutional changes that work to thoroughly institutionalize the military role in domestic and foreign affairs. Even if civilian rule returns, it may not matter all that much because the military is so tightly tied to the largest, most effective, and most prestigious institutions of the nation.

In addition to the many military problems that could grow out of a nuclear and technology arms race between Pakistan and India, the acceleration or unleashing of the increased administrative abilities of their military institutions is something that could have even more long-term effects, precisely because the capacity of civilian institutions is so limited. Such a transformation in India is the long-standing nightmare of civilian rulers in Delhi. It would threaten their democracy, a system not nearly as robust as those of the United States, Britain, or France.

The role of technology in the military organization of advanced Asian states is likely to be quite different than in developing nations because of the strength of other non-military institutions. Nonetheless, it is still a fruitful subject for exploration. In the case of Japan the military has almost no role in shaping foreign or domestic policy. Tokyo has military forces designed for self-defense, and there is virtually no evidence of any shift toward increased militarism. Indeed, available evidence points in the other direction. Despite increased spending on military forces, and a passing of the symbolic one-percent of GNP marker, Japan has trouble recruiting forces and the status of the military is, if anything, declining.

Yet the influence of the military in Japan is important because it is latent and this, in turn, affects the organization of Japanese forces. It has been argued that the Japanese political system produces a situation where no one is really in charge. A lack of central direction and a dispersion of authority make it difficult for Japanese prime ministers to control government agencies. The Japanese NSC system was modeled after the US one; Its actual role has been to limit the power of the Prime Minister by increasing the number of restrictions placed on his decision-making authority, the very opposite of the American system.

Were the military in Japan ever to increase their organizational capacity, the argument goes, it could lead to creation of an institution beyond the control of the executive and beyond the reach of public opinion.10 Whether or not this argument is exaggerated is an open question, but there can be little doubt that the military high command is not well integrated, and that there is enormous political reluctance to permit this to happen. Japanese Defense Agency bureaus are organized to preclude concentration of authority in any one office, and the Joint Staff Office provides only minimal lateral coordination among the services rather than true integration.

The interesting development here is that Japan is importing a great deal of defense technology of a kind that does require greater integration of its high command. The new OTH-B radar, AWACS aircraft, Aegis ships, and other systems are all highly intensive in information technology. Integration is also occurring with American forces, and what is happening is a kind of electronic integration of the Japanese command system with that of the US CINCPAC. This is consistent with the foreign policies of the two nations. Yet it is interesting to view the effects of advanced military technology on Japanese military organization as a fusion mechanism for constructing binding ties with the United States. One effect of information technology can be to establish such electronic ties, ones which parallel far more loosely coupled political ones.

Implications and Conclusions

The proliferation of advanced military technology has consequences that are far more complicated than first appears to be the case. It is not that proliferation cannot produce changes in regional military balances. It clearly can. But it also can transform the core of the state's decision-making apparatus, leading to wide-ranging strategic and economic changes compared to what went before. These processes are not well understood, partly because they are difficult to assess, but also because the problem has not been studied very much. It deserves much more attention, and could be a rich source of future scholarship and analysis. For controlling the spread of nuclear, chemical, ballistic missile, and conventional weapons there are some worthwhile insights that arise from this kind of analysis.

It has long been recognized that national decisions are at the heart of proliferation, but despite this the greatest amount of attention, political effort, and research on these matters has focused on the power internationally established to stop the spread of these weapons. One of the reasons for this has been an inability to conceptualize the national decision-making process. So far, most analyses of this have relied on rational analysis of costs and benefits or armchair assessments of political psychology. Neither of these paths grasps the fact that such decisions revolve around political and military organizations, and that leaders stand in a unique position, at least in partial control of institutions that straddle domestic and international pastures of decisionmaking.

Specifically, an institutional approach can identify critical thresholds that complement the thresholds highlighted in the NPT, various safeguard systems, and other external mechanisms. Indian leaders will not fail to notice the potential consequences of expanding the capacity of India's military institutions. This may constitute a significant barrier to full-scale deployment of certain kinds of military systems. Indeed, this has already happened; the Indian nuclear program has consciously avoided excessive influence of the military, in contrast to Pakistan. A better understanding of these *internal* thresholds could be a very useful complement to the study of external ones. It may be that we are overestimating the effectiveness of a non-proliferation regime conceived mainly by the United States and European countries for application in places with very different institutions and cultures. These places may possess their own powerful internal obstacles to proliferation, and it is important to understand them. Even in a country like North Korea, expanding the capacity and status of the army is something that may be a mixed blessing from the perspective of the senior leadership.

It is not that such internal thresholds can be expected to be binding, although they will influence the shape of any proliferation that comes. States may be content with the political benefits of possessing certain weapons, and reluctant to integrate them into their military forces. If they are integrated, more reliance may be placed on special purpose units, with tactical consequences. The Argentine Air Force performed rather well with their Exocet missile attacks on the British during the Falklands War. But there had been no practised coordination with the Argentine Army and there was no exploitation of the attacks. In the North Korean case, it may well be that the sum of the military forces is not nearly as effective as standard— that is, institution free—military balance analyses suggest. This is not to minimize the danger that exists on the Korean peninsula. On the contrary, the existence of major organizational seams in the North Korean armed forces may make the situation there even more dangerous, but in a different way.

Finally, there are implications for the US military role in Asia. In the past, the United States conceived its role in terms of the national strategy of containment of communist influence. The import of this was to conceptualize various combinations and packages for deterrence and war fighting by tipping regional balances in our favor through our technological military advantage. In the future, our ability to continue to operate in this way is in doubt. Not only will the United States have fewer forces deployed in Asia but, more fundamentally, there do not appear to be potential wars on the horizon (outside of Korea) that would involve us in operations. We will increasingly have to work *through* Asian military institutions to reach our goals. This means understanding them better: how they work, their role as political institutions, their use of technology, and their civil-military relations. One US role in Asia, then, could resemble our military ties to Latin America in the 1960s. Expanded training between the US military and its counterparts in Asia through educational exchanges and other programs could create a unique kind of "presence," one that would complement air, sea, and ground deployments. Increased military to military contact between the United States and Asian military organizations could give America access to important political and state making processes in Asia, in a way that is economical and fits the new security environment there.

NOTES

1. A review of the past pattern of the effects of nuclearization is found in Lewis A. Dunn and Sharon Squassoni, *Advanced Nuclear Weapon Proliferation: Some Lessons from the Past,* McLean, VA; Science Applications International Inc., 12, January 1990.

2. For a related discussion see Charles Tilly, *Coercion, Capital, and European States, AD 990-1990* (Oxford: Basil Blackwell, 1990), pp. 192–225.

3. S.E. Finer, *The Man on Horseback* (Boulder, CO: Westview Press, 1988).

4. Suck-Ho Lee, *Party-Military Relations in North Korea* (Seoul: Center for Peace and Unification of Korea, 1989).

5. Reinhard Drifte, "High Technology in the Japanese-American Defense Relationship and Northeast Asia," *The Korean Journal of Defense Analysis* (Winter 1989): pp. 77–103.

6. The argument for this relationship is advanced in Roman Kolkowicz as a general proposition and in the case of the Soviet Union in *The Soviet Military and the Communist Party* (Princeton, N.J.: Princeton University Press, 1967), pp. 34–35.

7. See Dale R. Herspring, "Technology and Civil-Military Relations: The Polish and East German Cases," in Dale R. Herspring and Ivan Volgyes, eds., *Civil-Military Relations in Communist Systems* (Boulder, CO: Westview Press, 1978), pp. 123–43.

8. See William H. McNeill, *The Pursuit of Power* (Chicago, IL: University of Chicago Press, 1982); and David B. Ralston, *Importing the European Army* (Chicago, IL: University of Chicago Press, 1990).

9. The Inter-Services Intelligence Directorate is described in George Arney, *Afghanistan* (London: Mandarin Books, 1990).

10. See Karel Von Wolferen, "Why Militarism Still Haunts Japan," *New York Times,* 22 December 1990, p. A23.

The World from a Pacific Perspective

PACIFIC ASIA AFTER THE OIL CRISIS AND US RECESSION: LESSONS IN RESILIENCE

Dr. William H. Overholt

Dr. William H. Overholt *graduated from Harvard and holds graduate degrees from Yale. He is presently Regional Strategist and a director of Bankers Trust Securities (Pacific). He has served as political adviser to several of Asia's major political figures. Before taking his post in Hong Kong, Dr. Overholt headed global political risk analysis for Bankers Trust, New York. Dr. Overholt also worked at the Hudson Institute for eight years and has directed political-military planning studies for various US government agencies. He is co-author of **Political Risk** and **Strategic Planning and Forecasting.***

The Pacific Asian economic miracle is now one generation old for most of the region's economies and nearly two generations old for some. Average growth for South Korea, Taiwan, Hong Kong, the Philippines, Thailand, Indonesia, Singapore, and Malaysia has been 7 percent compounded since 1960. Thailand has grown at that rate since World War II. Such a rate is more than three times what Britain achieved in the wake of the Industrial Revolution, which was the economic foundation of the British Empire. It is two to three times the rate that established the industrial foundations of today's big powers.

Superior economic performance sustained over an indefinite period of time leads inexorably to strategic superiority. Faster growth over a long period of time means faster technological progress, and faster technological progress eventually creates an ability to defeat the military technology of a slower economy. This does not mean that such a process occurs overnight. It can take many, many generations. And the slow emergence of economic/technological superiority can be interrupted by a military clash. But the inexorable connection between long-term economic superiority and long-term strategic superiority means that strategists of national power must take an interest in economic performance.

Contemporary geopolitics is dominated by two trends. The first is the collapse of the socialist economies, and with it their strategic position, in the face of superior competition from the market economies. The second is the gradual rise of the Pacific Asian economies compared with their weaker market-oriented competitors elsewhere.

Already the Pacific Asian economies (excluding the Philippines, which is structured more like a Latin American society) have so surpassed their Latin American and African competitors that one can no longer speak of a single Third World, comprising Africa, Asia, and Latin America. Pacific Asia is now clearly in a separate class. Already leaders in major Western capitals are wondering whether their economies and technologies can keep pace with Japanese advances. The smaller Asian economies have been growing considerably faster than Japan's, and their share of world trade surpassed Japan's in 1980 and has been rising faster ever since.

Many Western thinkers have taken solace from the view that the Asian takeoff is temporary and highly dependent upon the sufferance of Western policies. Thus, for instance, Herman Kahn's *The Emerging Japanese Superstate,* which argued the long-term strategic importance of Japan's economic growth, was quickly contradicted by Zbigniew Brzezinski's *The Fragile Blossom,* which argued that Japan's differences from the West made it an unsustainable hothouse flower. More generally, it has been argued over the years that Asia's superior growth rates were dependent on low energy prices, low interest rates, the rapid growth of Western markets, and easy access to Western markets. According to this view, when the United States catches cold, Asia should catch pneumonia.

If such a view is correct, we should be heading into a period of pneumonia for Asian societies, After all, the United States is in recession, there is a risk of very high oil prices if the Gulf War takes an unexpected turn, and Western protectionism has crept to fairly severe levels and could become much more severe during a recession after the breakdown of the Uruguay Round. But the evidence reviewed below indicates that, on the contrary, Pacific Asia will do very well indeed; when the United States catches pneumonia, Asia only catches cold.

Previous Oil Crisis/Recession Combination

We have been through combinations of oil crisis and recession before. Oil prices rose drastically in 1973 and 1978, and recessions occurred in 1974–75, 1980, and 1982. To understand the future, we can most efficiently begin by reviewing analogies from the past.

Past oil crises were far more severe (involving a sustained quadrupling of oil prices) than the nineties' brief doubling of oil prices. Pacific Asian countries should be terribly vulnerable to oil price rises, much more so than the United States, because Japan, South Korea, Taiwan, Singapore, the Philippines, and Thailand have negligible domestic energy supplies. As Table I shows, the 1973 oil price rise caused a short recession in Japan and a long recession in the United States, but no recession at all in the dynamic smaller Pacific Asian economies. To be sure, growth declined in 1974 and 1975, but it declined to a level of about twice what would be considered a very good rate in the United States. (Most economists view 2.5 percent as about the limit of what the United States can sustain without generating serious inflation.)

Table I
ECONOMIC PERFORMANCE DURING THE FIRST OIL CRISIS
(% real GNP growth rate)

	1973	1974	1975	1976
United States	5.2	− 0.5	− 1.3	4.9
Japan	7.9	− 1.4	2.7	4.8
Hong Kong	12.7	2.2	0.2	17.1
Malaysia	11.7	8.3	0.8	11.6
Singapore	11.5	6.3	4.1	8.4
Indonesia	11.3	7.6	5.0	6.7
Philippines	10.1	5.6	5.8	7.4
Thailand	9.4	5.5	7.1	8.7
South Korea	14.4	7.9	4.4	13.7
Taiwan	12.8	7.2	4.4	13.7

The year 1975 is particularly interesting because it combines the full impact of the first oil crisis with the full impact of a serious US recession. In that year, most Pacific Asian economies grew more than 4 percent, a level the United States rarely reaches, and the two that grew below 1 percent, namely Hong Kong and Malaysia, bounced back the following year to 17.1 and 11.6 percent respectively.

A similar pattern emerged after the second oil crisis in 1978. In 1979, no Pacific Asian economy grew less that 5.3 percent, more than double a good year for the United States, and most grew far faster than that, with Hong Kong at 11.7 percent leading the group and Malaysia and Singapore close behind at 9.3 and 9.4 percent respectively.

Table II
GDP, GNP PERFORMANCE DURING THE SECOND OIL CRISIS
(REAL % CHANGE)

	1979	1980	1981
Japan	5.3	4.3	3.7
United Kingdom	2.1	− 2.1	− 1.1
United States	2.5	− 0.2	1.9
Hong Kong	11.7	10.9	9.4
Malaysia	9.3	7.4	6.9
Singapore	9.4	9.7	9.6
Indonesia	6.3	9.9	7.9
Philippines	6.9	5.0	3.4
Thailand	5.3	4.8	6.3
South Korea	7.2	− 3.7	5.9
Taiwan	8.5	7.1	5.3

The following year, 1980, again combined the effects of oil crisis and US recession but no dynamic Pacific Asian economy, except South Korea, grew less than 4.8 percent and most were in the 7 to 11 percent range. South Korea was an exception not because of oil crisis and recession but rather because of the aftermath of Park Chung Hee's October 1979 assassination and of severe domestic inflation.)

The 1982 Recession

Two years later, in 1982, came the worst recession since the Great Depression. This Great Recession was a particularly severe test of the dynamic Asian economies, because those economies are driven by exports and 1982 saw the first decline in world trade since World War II. Clearly, such a year ought to be devastating, particularly for a country like Singapore, whose total trade (exports plus imports) usually exceeds three hundred percent of GNP. It is therefore astounding that none of these economies experienced a recession and all but Indonesia grew more than 3 percent that year. Singapore, the most trade-dependent, grew 6.9 percent.

Oil Crisis Adaptations

The Pacific Asian trading economies manage an oil crisis by passing through much of the oil price rise to consumers of their exports and by adapting faster than their competitors. First, they pass much of the cost through: Hong Kong imports a cup of oil and exports a plastic flower. The rise in the world

ASIAN GROWTH 1982
(The Great Recession)

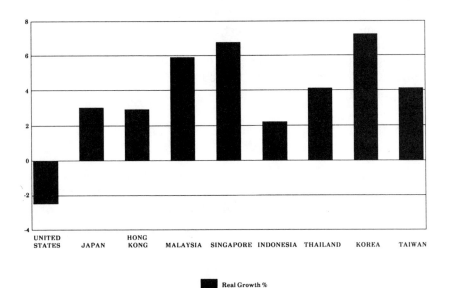

Real Growth %

Asian Growth, 1982

market price of the plastic flowers generally pays for the increased price of the oil. South Korea does the same with plastics, petrochemicals, and steel (which has a high energy content). Singapore, a huge oil importer, consumes only 10 percent of its imported oil. It refines and exports the remaining 90 percent, and because the refining process adds so much value Singapore actually comes out ahead: if oil prices rise from $18 to $25, then Singapore's imports go up 7.1 percent but its exports rise 8.2 percent.

Second, and more important, the dynamic Pacific Asian economies typically adjust faster than Western economies. For instance, after the first oil crisis the US government held down fuel prices artificially until 1980; as a direct consequence, efforts by American automobile companies to market small, fuel-efficient cars failed. In contrast, countries like South Korea forced gasoline prices above market levels in order to stimulate rapid adjustment and conservation. Japan adjusted quickly, and the resulting national demand for small, fuel-efficient cars was a principal reason for the rapid Japanese takeover of this segment of the world market. Similar phenomena have given Pacific Asian countries special advantages in most of the products they export.

One can easily rank the Asian countries in terms of their ability to pass energy costs through to other consumers and their political will to adjust.

- Indonesia and Malaysia are oil exporters, so they do not face adjustment problems.

- Singapore and Hong Kong have tiny populations with limited transport and agricultural fertilizer requirements, so they pass the highest proportion of their costs on to foreign consumers; they also adjust virtually instantly.

- Taiwan and South Korea have larger populations, with greater transport and fertilizer consumption, but they too adjust instantly and often "over-adjust" as their governments seek to force rapid adaptation to market requirements.

- Thailand, geographically and demographically the size of France, has very large transportation and fertilizer consumption, and its more representative politics (even in periods of military rule) slow down its adjustments as compared with Taiwan and South Korea in the 1970s and 1980s, but it still adjusts more decisively than the United States because of the influence of its technocratic bureaucracies.

- The Philippines has a large population and territory, and therefore consumes large amounts of energy in transportation and agriculture. Its economy has not developed as the others have, so it lacks energy-intensive exports that would pass on the costs to foreigners. (The main Philippine exports are sugar, coconuts, and copper.) Populist politics in the Philippines slows the adjustment process, so that the country faces a debt crisis rather than an opportunity.

This priority for short-term political considerations over long-term economic considerations is the essence of the difference between Asian economic performance on one hand and Latin American/Philippine economic performance on the other. The United States lies somewhere in between these two extremes, but has been evolving slowly away from the Asian end of the spectrum as immediate populist pressures erode the role of the political party elders in choosing presidential candidates, as populist "reforms" erode the importance of seniority in the Congress, and as television sound bytes gradually gain influence as compared with reasoned debate in political campaigns.

The Philippine case is profoundly instructive. The priority for short-term political considerations overwhelms economic management, in sharp contrast to neighboring Asian societies. Rather than instituting effective land reform, the Philippine government allows landlord pressures to emasculate its program. Rather than reducing the exchange rate to encourage exports, the Philippine government bows to elite demands for cheap imports and keeps the exchange rate overvalued. Rather than reforming the civil service and the military, it worsens the situation as an accommodation to political demands for patronage. Rather than reducing tariffs decisively, it delays tariff reform and uses the excuse of oil prices to reinstate high tariffs. Rather than raising taxes and reducing expenditures to resolve a budget crisis, it waits until a foreign debt crisis and overwhelming foreign financial pressures force limited reforms. The consequence is low growth, high inflation, and financial crisis in a region marked by high growth, relatively controlled inflation, and financial abundance. (Japan and Taiwan have the world's largest foreign exchange reserves, and the fast growing countries have virtually eliminated their foreign debts.)

The Philippines has population, territory, cultural, and natural resource endowments very similar to Thailand's. It entered the modern period with vastly superior infrastructure, education, and per capita income—as well as with vastly superior democracy. But it lacked a structure of powerful technocratic institutions that could channel or sometimes override populist pressures when those pressures were not in the long-term national interest. (Thailand faced far worse initial economic circumstances, but spent decades building technocratic institutions that could manage the country's economy and security properly, then liberalized its politics to the extent that seemed consistent with sound economic and security management.) The result, aggravated but not caused by the era of Marcos mismanagement, has been the Philippines' loss of its preeminent economic position among the smaller Asian economies and its decline in a series of economic crises. This threatens not just the economy but also the democracy: the most recent official Philippine public opinion polls show public support for President Aquino at a far lower level than the worst under Marcos just before the 1986 revolution; they also show rising discontent with democracy. In contrast, recent Thai economic performance has been spectacular, and the end-of-February coup is likely just to correct some excesses; it is part of a political-military cycle in which there is a strong long-term tendency, punctuated by occasional setbacks, toward political democratization and liberalization.

Sources of Superior Adjustment

The superior adjustment capabilities of the dynamic Pacific Asian economies derive from several sources. The discussion above has alluded to the most important of these, namely an ingrained emphasis on long-term economic considerations at the expense of short-term political ones. This, in turn, derived from fear: North Korea's fear of South Korea, Taiwan's and Hong Kong's fear of China, Singapore's fear of Indonesia and Malaysia, Japan's postwar humiliation and fear that it would be unable to recover. All reached—by different routes—the same conclusion, namely, that national salvation lay only in superior long-term economic performance, at great cost in terms of rapid political liberalization, traditional obligations to family and friends, and short-term political popularity of the leadership. The Philippines failed to find the path to these conclusions because it gained independence without sacrifice and continued to be sheltered by the United States from all important risks, including the risks consequent upon the political elite's own follies, long after independence.

Another way of saying the same thing is that the successful countries are determined that the national interest will dominate the sectional interest, that, for instance, the overall economy will not be held hostage to the interests of textile producers or motorists. This is not to say that these economies lack patronage or politically-motivated economic policies; the exclusions that protect Japanese and Korean rice producers are among the thousands of examples of inefficient patronage policies. But what is noteworthy among the successful Pacific Asian countries is not the prevalence of such policies, which are universal, but the determination and steadiness of the drive toward more competitive and efficient policies over the decades. This produces startling gains in productivity—from the Japanese opening of financial markets to the Indonesian opening of import markets. The difference between Asian success and Latin American failure is the power of the Asian drive for productivity gains.

Closely related to this priority for productivity is the reconciliation by these governments of a powerful government role in the economy with a market-driven economy. Each of the successful Pacific Asian governments plays a larger role in its economy than Washington does in the American economy, but their economies adjust more rapidly to market conditions than the US economy. In short, they have resolved the issue that has long divided Democratic proponents of big government from Republican proponents of market forces. How is this possible? The answer is logically trivial but politically profound: these governments define their role primarily (not exclusively, but primarily) in terms of facilitating adjustment to market conditions rather than fighting the markets. When the low-end textile industry becomes obsolete for their economic conditions, the Japanese and Taiwan governments facilitate its departure to countries with cheaper labor, thereby freeing up their own labor and other resources for more productive activity. In contrast, the US government bows to pressure groups and encourages obsolete economic activity, so the trend for more than a decade has been steadily in the wrong direction. When oil prices rise, South Korea and Taiwan force rapid adjustment instead of inhibiting it. And so forth.

Several of the most successful countries, Japan, South Korea, and Taiwan, have also managed to reconcile rapid growth with egalitarian income distribution. Again, they have reconciled what Western analysts and politicians have long believed to be incompatible. The Kuznets curve was long believed to demonstrate that high growth in the middle period of development was achievable only at the cost of severe income maldistribution. Republicans and Democrats, conservatives and social democrats have long been divided over the relative priority between expanding the economy and dividing the shares equally. Now we have Asian economies that grow 7 to 10 percent annually and divide the pie more evenly than Sweden. They have not done this through magic, but rather by combining the wisdom of both right and left: land reform, luxury taxes, universal education, and labor intensive industry in order to achieve egalitarian income distributions; competition, increasing openness, competitive exchange rates, and market prices for labor to promote growth. They have avoided the trap of the West and the South whereby a premature emphasis on heavy industry creates economic pressures for slow growth and inequality, while a political coalition of heavy industry, a labor elite, and a political class delivers above-market wages (usually via a minimum wage law and other ostensibly egalitarian measures) to a small proportion of the workforce at the expense of massive unemployment.

ASIAN SOCIAL INNOVATIONS
(PREDOMINANTLY NORTHEAST ASIA)

- LONG-TERM ECONOMICS DOMINATES POLITICS
- NATIONAL INTEREST DOMINATES SECTIONAL
- MARKET IS RECONCILED WITH STRONG GOVERNMENT
- LABOR DISCIPLINE, PRODUCTIVITY, RAPID WAGE GROWTH ARE RECONCILED
- STRONG GOVERNMENT IS RECONCILED WITH LIMITED BUDGET
- STRONG MILITARY IS RECONCILED WITH LIMITED BUDGET

The Pacific Asian countries have also proceeded far toward reconciling labor discipline, smooth labor-management relations, rapid productivity growth, and rapid wage growth. In most countries, including Japan, this reconciliation started in a way that did not look like a reconciliation: the kinds of confrontational unionism that the West takes for granted were simply suppressed. South Korea and Taiwan are only now emerging from this relatively unpleasant period of labor-management relations. But out of early suppression has grown a virtuous circle in which low wages and rapidly rising productivity create high growth and low employment and, eventually, labor scarcity and rapidly rising wages. Rapid wage increases then begin to make cooperation with management more attractive, and a mutually beneficial circle of cooperation develops. This virtuous circle is not a product of ancient philosophies and exotic management practices but rather is a consequence of having created a rapidly growing pie and being willing to share it. Under Park Chung Hee and Roh Tae Woo (although not under Chun Doo Hwan), South Korean wages grew at rates unheard of in any period of American history. Other successful Asian economies are following similar paths. American unions' protests about Asian "sweatshops" generally choose not to emphasize this point.

Likewise, efficient use of people and rapidly growing productivity have enabled such governments as Japan, South Korea, and Taiwan to achieve very powerful and effective government while using a very limited percentage of the population as government officials and a relatively small fraction of GNP as government revenue.

Finally, a matter of crucial importance to this audience: a rapidly growing economy makes possible a very rapid rise in military strength while using only a limited share of GNP for military purposes. Japan is the most extreme example, with an increasingly impressive military machine gradually evolving from expenditure of only 1 percent of GNP. But Japan is only the most extreme example, and Japan's semi-pacifist philosophy need not be part of this approach to long-term strategy. In the Kennedy years, the US military received 9–10 percent of GNP while the South Korean military, arguably the most threatened in the world, received only about 4 percent. At the time, the North Korean military hugely overshadowed its southern counterpart. But because of superior economic growth the South Korean military today is gradually surpassing with 6 percent of GNP its North Korean counterpart which is spending over 30 percent.

Broader Crisis Resilience

This analysis has focused on the Asian economies' response to a current situation of oil crisis and US recession. But the resilience of Asian economies is not limited to such situations. The sources of resilience noted above are broadly applicable to a vast range of different stresses in the world economy. Their superior ability to adapt to new circumstances is a broad capability rooted in government determination to channel the tides of history rather than fight them, and in social structures that are more cooperative than is common in the West. To this must be added that Asian economies are no longer dependent on Western financing and technology to the extent they were a generation ago; instead, Japan and Taiwan are financing the United States, and several Asian economies are on the verge of challenging the United States in some of the highest areas of technology.

Asian economies are also becoming less dependent on generous access to Western markets than is widely believed. Gradual creeping protectionism meets effective responses: South Korea meets quotas on shoes by moving up-market from sandals to designer shoes, so that revenue continues to rise at a rapid rate even if volume is flat. Japan meets restrictions on automobile exports by building factories in the United States. The burden of spreading protectionism falls disproportionately on those whose political systems render them less capable of rapid adjustment, namely the Third World outside Pacific Asia and to some extent the Western countries themselves. And Asia is increasingly providing markets for itself: the leading Asian economies now grow predominantly through domestic growth, and the 1990s will likely see intra-Asian trade exceed trans-Pacific trade.

The depth of Asian crisis resilience can be measured by looking at what happened in the early 1980s, when the world economy suffered from the highest energy prices, the worst recession, the highest interest rates in modern history, some of the worst currency fluctuations in modern history, the worst Third World debt crisis in all of history, and a contraction of world trade. Pacific Asian economies that were trade-dependent, energy-import-dependent, and heavily indebted should logically have been devastated. Instead, their market share of world trade grew at about four times the rate that they had achieved during the previous two decades of better times. When the going gets tough, the tough get going.

Some Implications

This analysis has important strategic implications. First, superior Asian growth is not going to be halted by fluctuations in the economic environment. The dynamic Pacific Asian economies have achieved a crisis resilience that is broadly applicable to a wide range of stresses in the world economy and that derives from social and political innovations rather than from temporary economic conditions.

Second, Pacific Asian advantages derive from institutions and practices that are not particularly esoteric, but the West appears to have great difficulty learning to emulate them or to innovate effective responses that would restore Western competitiveness. Unless the West does innovate appropriate responses, this will lead eventually to a decisive shift in the global strategic balance.

Third, turning inward will simply accelerate the West's loss of strategic position. There are many historical precedents for this. Regions of the world which responded to the industrial revolution by trying to isolate themselves from it invariably found themselves subordinated to countries which embraced it. The Islamic world, once the center of world culture, commerce, and power, lost power, wealth and cultural attractiveness when it turned inward. China, which for longer periods than any other country was the world's pinnacle of prosperity and technology, became impotent and impoverished when it responded to Western challenge by seeking to isolate itself.

These analogies may seem far-fetched, but it is a mistake to think that the fundamental lessons of history, and of competitive economics, do not apply to ourselves. It would be a fundamental error not to see that the ability to grow two to three times as fast generation after generation constitutes a fundamental challenge. It would be an equally fundamental error to take comfort in comparatively minor historical differences in order to avoid these lessons. The Asian countries have learned some logically simple but politically difficult lessons about resilient management that we ignore at our peril.

CHINA AND JAPAN IN THE NEW PACIFIC ERA

Dr. Jonathan D. Pollack

Dr. Jonathan D. Pollack is corporate research manager for international policy at the RAND Corporation and also heads the International Policy Department. Dr. Pollack holds M.A. and Ph.D. degrees from the University of Michigan. He has been a post-doctoral fellow at Harvard University and taught at Brandeis University. A specialist in Chinese, Sino-Soviet, and US-China relations, Dr. Pollack has published widely. His recent studies include **US Strategic Alternatives in a Changing Pacific**, and **Into the Vortex: China, the Sino-Soviet Alliance and the Korean War.**

The stunning reconfiguration of the international system over the past several years leaves global and regional political alignments more unsettled than at any time since the end of World War II. The decisive defeat of Iraqi forces in Kuwait is only the most recent development in a sequence of events that began with the collapse of Soviet power in Eastern Europe and the consequent breakdown of the Cold War system; these transformations have yet to abate.

Few observers seem perspicacious enough to see an end to this process of international change. Too much seems contingent in any forecast, especially in the context of the highly unsettled internal politics of a number of major international actors. In the aftermath of the Gulf crisis, the expectations of sustained comity between the Soviet Union and the United States also appear inflated. Expectations that the emergence of Germany and Japan would inevitably translate into a multipolar world and a diminished role for American power seem comparably premature. The reverberations of the crisis in the Gulf will be felt for years and possibly decades, as the United States and its coalition partners seek, at great cost and effort, to achieve stability and security in a region of exceptional volatility and strategic importance. Indeed, even as the projection of American power was decisive to the outcome in the Gulf, these events could not have transpired without the political, economic, and military support provided by others who also saw their vital interests at risk. The United States may now appear to many observers the only comprehensive global power, but it cannot exercise its power unilaterally, nor can it expect that other actors will obligingly consent to a single vision of international peace and security in the 1990s.

The Persian Gulf crisis also suggests that the "post-Cold War world" may be more unstable and violence-prone than the bipolar framework that preceded it. The US-Soviet rivalry in Europe and East Asia—ratified by American and Soviet nuclear forces—inhibited either state from acting militarily in a way that could draw the other into direct armed conflict; it also cautioned the military behavior of other states. Not surprisingly, violence in the international system over the past 40 years has been in various Third World locales where the possibility of escalation to major power war generally appeared remote; should the inhibitions on the use of force relax significantly, then the resort to force in local or regional settings could become a staple of global politics in the 1990s and beyond.

Thus, estimates on the future of the international strategic system must remain somewhat cautionary. The world is not necessarily on the verge of an anarchic war of all against all. Many forces seem likely to mitigate various political or military tensions, and some regions are assuredly more stable than others. Much seems likely to depend on the character and consequences of any realignment of political forces, and the capacity of regional actors to collaborate intelligently to avoid debilitating rivalries. The robustness, consistency, and self-confidence with which various major powers can exercise their influence will also matter a great deal. Without question, however, a world appreciably loosened from the moorings of the long dominant Soviet-US framework could prove a far more complex and less predictable place. To grasp some of these possibilities as they could apply in Asia and the Pacific, we need to consider the geopolitical inheritance from the past several decades, and what they may imply about the future.

Identifying East Asia's Strategic Patterns

This essay explores future strategic configurations in East Asia and their potential effects on relations between China and Japan.[1] The two states appear in almost all estimates of a world with multiple major powers. Despite the cant of an "emergent multipolar world," there is very little consensus among scholars or practitioners about alternative strategic futures in East Asia and their security implications.[2] Thus, there is no intrinsic logic or inevitable direction to future Sino-Japanese political and security calculations; they assume significance only in relation to prevailing and future strategic patterns.

Three broad trends have shaped major power interactions in East Asia since the late 1960s: first, the augmentation of Soviet military power on the Asian mainland and in the

Pacific; second, the application of extended US deterrence commitments, most prominently in the US-Japan alliance but extending to other regional actors; and, third, China's pursuit of an autonomous political-military capability. Each merits discussion.

In the late 1960s, Moscow began a sustained buildup of Soviet ground, air, and strategic forces opposite China. A parallel modernization and enhancement of Soviet naval strength, although related to Sino-Soviet tensions, addressed the security challenge posed by the offshore US naval and air presence. Moscow's buildup reflected the globalization of Soviet military power. The Soviets did not choose between east and west: they deployed major military forces simultaneously in both Europe and Asia.

The seemingly inexorable quality of Soviet military modernization therefore contributed to the Sino-American accommodation, while also enabling a step-by-step enhancement of US-Japanese security arrangements. The United States did not have to choose between extensive relations with Japan and much enhanced political and economic ties with China. At the same time, Beijing was prepared to tacitly endorse the US military presence in East Asia, including the US-Japan alliance. Chinese incentives to collaborate with Japan also grew, although these did not extend to meaningful security collaboration.[3]

China's vulnerability to Soviet power and America's desire to counterbalance Soviet capabilities provided a political logic for Chinese security strategy. Although Beijing sought to avoid overly encumbering relations with any major power, necessity and practical interests dictated collaboration with the United States and political restraint toward Japan. In the late 1970s and early 1980s, the Chinese also openly encouraged Japan to enhance its military power, hoping to further complicate Soviet strategic designs.

The United States was thus able to sustain mutually reinforcing relations with Tokyo and Beijing, with the Soviet Union denied a credible political or economic relationship with either. Chinese opportunities for collaboration with the region's market economies also increased, as did its incentives for political restraint on issues where Chinese and American security interests were in conflict, as in Taiwan. At the same time, although Tokyo and Beijing remained ambivalent about the long-term implications of one another's power and national goals, near-term exigencies dictated heightened Japanese involvement in China's national development plans. The United States encouraged such collaboration, but expectations of US-Japanese-Chinese security coordination were more notional than real. Only in the late 1970s, when China advocated an anti-Soviet "united front" strategy to escape its own isolation and to deny Moscow a potential political bridgehead along the Pacific rim, was there ever a putative strategic pattern, and it was not long-lived. Even so, the Chinese remained for a time active and explicit in their solicitation of relations with Japanese military officers, with officials in Tokyo far more reluctant to engage in activities that appeared overly collaborative or formalized.[4]

The normalization of Sino-Soviet relations, however, helped transform the security framework of East Asia. In essence, the Soviet Union is no longer prepared to sustain an open-ended military confrontation with the PRC, and the Chinese have responded to this opportunity. Although Sino-Soviet relations retain elements of conflict and uncertainty, the two sides appear prepared to pare back their past military deployments on a step-by-step basis, and have undertaken negotiations on the reduction of military forces, consultations on Asia-Pacific security issues, and the resumption of Sino-Soviet military relations after a hiatus of nearly three decades. Thus, the logic of a "strategic triangle" seems largely irrelevant to Soviet-US-Chinese dynamics in the 1990s.[5]

At the same time, there are major uncertainties about the sustainability of the American regional security role. The United States is now less prepared to assume a disproportionate responsibility for its Asian allies, a tendency reinforced by mounting US budgetary constraints. This trend could well be accelerated by the more immediate demands imposed by the hostilities in Southwest Asia and the need to devise a viable, longer-term security strategy for the Gulf region. Nationalistic grievances within East Asia, most notably in the Philippines, are further calling into question the capability of the United

States to maintain access to bases and facilities upon which the forward deployment of US naval and air power depend. At the same time, the United States has placed increased pressure on its more prosperous regional allies to contribute to global rather than local security requirements, most recently in the Persian Gulf. The future role of Japan, and the extent to which it assumes added responsibility for security either in Northeast Asia or in other locales, has therefore emerged among the pivotal issues in East Asia's future. We thus need to explore Chinese evaluations of the shifting security environment, in particular as they pertain to Japan.

Japan in the Emergent Security Environment— Some Views from Beijing

Since the mid-1980s, there has been a gradual Chinese reassessment of Japan's role in the international system and its implications for China's regional position. In late 1984, Pei Monong, a leading Chinese international affairs researcher, transposed the logic of PRC security strategy onto economic relations among the United States, Japan, and the ASEAN states. He described Washington and Tokyo as "economic superpowers" (*jingji chaoji daguo*) who colluded and competed for economic domination. Although ASEAN was the putative battleground of this rivalry for economic supremacy, Pei's analysis comported with China's efforts to maneuver for advantage between Washington and Moscow. In his paper, China (that is, ASEAN) by implication, would be the object of solicitation by both superpowers, thereby building its indigenous strength in the process.[6]

Pei's analysis foreshadowed subsequent Chinese efforts to reconceptualize East Asian security. However, so long as Chinese analysts asserted that the US-Soviet strategic rivalry for global domination remained undiminished, there was no possibility of an alternative formula giving primacy (or at least enhanced importance) to regional powers such as China. [7] Subsequent Chinese assessments underscored an inescapable fact: a prospective multipolar system entailed the emergence of *both* China and Japan as major powers in Asia, with Tokyo having a far more legitimate claim to this status and to American attention. Thus, the Chinese, long accustomed to Tokyo's subordinate political status in the Japanese-American alliance and to its highly equivocal exercise of political power, have been compelled to assess the implications of a Japan with a larger stake and responsibilities in the emergent structure of international power. This had led Beijing to rethink its previous (if somewhat understated) endorsement of a larger Japanese defense effort.

The steady enhancement of Japanese power (including military power) has been an especially troubling development to numerous Chinese strategic observers, particularly since it has seemed largely independent of the late 1980s' shift toward a more collaborative Soviet-US relationship. Japan's announcement in January 1987 that its defense expenditure would surpass one percent of GNP constituted a symbolic threshold for the Chinese, as well. This announcement triggered strong responses from Beijing, including an attribution to Japan of larger political ambitions.[8] Nearly all subsequent Chinese commentaries have expressed varying degrees of reservation about the increase of Japanese defense capabilities and its longer-term consequences. Although some commentaries have viewed Japanese defense expenditure, and the corollary effort by Japan to assume increased security responsibility, as largely a response to pressure from the United States, the practical implications seem worrisome: they bespeak the emergence of a more powerful and potentially more assertive Japanese state.

By late 1987, therefore, Japan's enhanced defense efforts were deemed unambiguous evidence of Japanese ambitions as a "political power."[9] Although Chinese commentaries were undoubtedly intended to caution Japan, they also appeared to reflect internal debate in Beijing about the sustainability of longer-term Sino-Japanese cooperation. When meeting with a delegation from *Asahi Shimbun* in February 1988, for example, Zhao Ziyang specifically urged "politicians of the two countries" to avoid overreactions to increased Sino-Japanese tensions, and to treat relations "from a longer-term standpoint."[10] However, during Japanese Prime Minister Takeshita's summer 1988 visit to China, Deng Xiaoping failed to raise any concerns about Japanese nationalism, enhanced Japanese defense expenditure, or various incidents in Japan that Beijing had previously deemed anti-Chinese.11 These somewhat mixed signals suggested a measure of uncertainty in Beijing about the appropriate response to Japanese policy developments.

But the coalescence of various political and military trends began to generate far greater momentum, direction, and specificity in Chinese commentaries. Whereas many earlier assessments were either brief newspaper items or informational presentations in military journals on specific weapons systems, by 1988-89 policy guidance permitted far more exhaustive treatment of Japan's military potential in authoritative publications. In January 1989, for example, *Guoji Wenti Yanjiu,* the quarterly publication of the Institute of International Studies of the Ministry of Foreign Affairs, published an extraordinarily detailed assessment of Japanese defense policy and military capabilities.12 The article undoubtedly drew on detailed military intelligence assessments and estimates, revealing a heretofore undisclosed effort to monitor the full range of Japanese defense programs and activities.

According to the author, Japanese defense concepts have evolved steadily from

> "defense in place," strictly limiting defense to Japan's soil ... and passively meeting an enemy attack, to serious attention to pre-combat preparations and achieving victory early in a war; from the idea of annihilating the enemy on the beaches to annihilating the enemy at sea; and from combat in coastal waters to combat on the high seas.

At the same time, the author asserted, the Japanese were also laying the foundation for far more elaborate high technology programs for national defense, including in space. These trends, in conjunction with a steady enhancement of US-Japanese defense collaboration to a distance of 1,000 nautical miles beyond Japan's home islands, demonstrated that past Japanese constitutional restraints on military activity "have gradually become dead letters, and their binding force weakened long ago." Moreover, such trends bespoke "the consequences of the nationalist ideological trend running wild." All such trends, the author further observed, were taking place at a time of diminished East-West tensions, and with growing pressures for reduction of military expenditures on a worldwide basis. Subsequent Chinese commentaries (including some since the Tiananmen crisis) have also asserted that the United States has simply goaded an already willing Japan, with Soviet military activities in Asia serving "as a major pretext for [Japanese] arms expansion."13

Other commentaries, however, have depicted US-Japanese relations, including security relations, in a more uncertain light. As observed by one Chinese military analyst, the United States, although seeking "to control Japan [and make] Japan its important strategic partner forever," was voicing a growing wariness about Japan's longer-term ambitions, including the tendency of "Japan taking the road of a military power."14 But these contradictions remain a longer-term "hidden danger," since Japan's defense capabilities are still very limited relative to those of the United States, as well as being subject to both political and economic constraints. Moreover, the author asserted, "the present Japan-US economic frictions have not yet reached the stage of endangering the strategic cooperation between both sides. To preserve their common strategic interests, both sides ... [are trying] to keep the frictions within the limit of the economic field and to avoid their development into political problems. The common strategic requirement will still be the basic factor for maintaining the relation of alliance between Japan and the US." According to an additional commentary in *Shijie Zhishi,* US-Japanese relations "have entered the most turbulent period in the postwar era, and Japan no longer plays the obedient lamb of the United States." However, in view of "its far from full-fledged military strength," Japan still requires security protection from the United States. At the same time, the author asserted, "the United States intends to restrict Japan in developing its defense forces and equipment, and to impede Japan in developing [an] arms system of its own." On balance, "although there are contradictions of sorts in US-Japanese relations, no radical change in the basic pattern of relations between the two countries is on the horizon in the foreseeable future."15

Thus, there appear to be competing impulses at work in Chinese assessments of Japan's power and future role. One current of opinion appears intent on drawing worst case (or near-worst case) estimates about Japan's ambitions and power potential, quite possibly for reasons that are institutional rather than being based on reasoned strategic assessment.16 Others, however, see Japan operating in somewhat constrained fashion, still dependent on American power and strategic protection, and with both Washington and Tokyo recognizing a huge shared stake in sustaining collaboration in all forms. But even the latter, less pessimistic school of thought, perceives latent contradictions that could over time increase. In the broadest sense, therefore, these assessments do not presage a highly stable outlook for the future US-Japanese relationship.

These issues all assumed far greater urgency in the context of the Persian Gulf crisis. The United States demonstrably solicited political support from the Chinese, especially in the context of the UN Security Council deliberations during the fall of 1990. But Japan was clearly deemed a more vital cog in US policy. American pressures on Japan to contribute economic and manpower support in the Gulf elicited predictable expressions of Chinese concern, although the inability or unwillingness of the Japanese to move decisively to support American policy may have tempered Chinese anxieties about Tokyo's global as well as regional responsibilities. But these trends underscore Chinese anxieties in an international strategic environment where Tokyo's policies assume greater centrality and consequence for peace and security than do those of Beijing.

The consequences of a larger Japanese international role are therefore potentially very worrisome to the Chinese, especially in the aftermath of China's internal political crisis of 1989. Japanese claims to enhanced international status, or the attribution of such a role to Japan by other states, impinge upon comparable Chinese pretensions. China's pursuit of an independent power position has presumed the readiness of the major powers to invest such prospective status in Beijing; to the extent that this attention is directed elsewhere, the implications of the diffusion of international power may be far less welcomed by the Chinese than their declaratory posture suggests.

Some Possible Scenarios

If the security structure of the past several decades will no longer characterize East Asian regional politics in the 1990s, what will supplant it? It is very difficult to offer precise forecasts, especially in an era that Chinese strategists appropriately deem one of profound but incomplete transformation.[17] Projections of the aggregate growth of economic, technological, and military capabilities tell part of the story,[18] but these do not translate into predictable power relationships, as distinct from power attributes. Once analysis admits to the possibility of multiple interactions less constrained by a bipolar framework, the political and strategic landscape becomes almost impossibly complex. The uncertain political and economic futures of the Soviet, Chinese, and North Korean systems render these estimates even more problematic.

For purposes of analysis, we will consider six potential patterns for East Asia's future. These scenarios are not all equally likely, but all are intuitively plausible. Four principal variables seem likely to determine which patterns will dominate:

- the extent of the breakdown of the cold war system in East Asia, and competition and cooperation that evolve from it;

- the persistence of US-Japanese political, economic, and security collaboration, as opposed to the emergence of overtly antagonistic relations;

- the readiness of the United States to continue its obligations to regional security (this consideration is closely related to the second factor); and

- the capacity of Leninist systems to remain economically and politically viable in a radically different international era.

Each of the patterns, in turn, has different implications for future Sino-Japanese relations, and the disposition of leaders in Beijing and Tokyo to treat the one another's power (especially military power) as threatening, mutually supportive, or largely benign.

Some cases have been excluded from this assessment, most notably scenarios for the Korean peninsula. This is a highly complex topic in its own right. Depending on various political outcomes in Pyongyang, for example, the two Koreas could:

- move rapidly toward unification;

- begin a step-by-step accommodation akin to relations between East Germany and West Germany in the early 1970s; or

- with the advent of a North Korean nuclear capability, make the military confrontation along the 38th Parallel even more explosive.

In a more near-term sense, it would appear that all the major powers are moving toward an avowed two-Koreas policy; declaratory policy notwithstanding, few voices appear intent on pushing too far or too fast toward Korean reunification. But the potential volatility on the peninsula underscores the highly contingent character of this exercise.

Case One: A Collaborative Multilateral System. The first case would entail realization of Deng Xiaoping's "new international political order." It assumes a non-antagonistic framework within which all major actors would enjoy mutually reinforcing collaborative relations. The resort to force and the deployment of military power beyond national borders would diminish sharply or disappear altogether. Deng's concept depicts the presumed objectives of Chinese international strategy during the 1980s—simultaneous, non-antagonistic relations between China and all major powers. However, the near-term prospects for realizing this goal evaporated amidst the carnage of Tiananmen and China's consequent estrangement from the industrialized world, especially the United States.

Even had there been no Tiananmen crisis, it is difficult to conceive of China operating as successfully in a world devoid of principal contradictions. Thus, Beijing has regularly advocated a far less antagonistic superpower relationship, but now confronts the possibility of Soviet-US collaboration that could consign China to a far more peripheral role in global and regional security arrangements. (As noted previously, however, these expectations appear premature in the aftermath of the rightward turn in Soviet internal politics and its consequent effects in the Gulf war.) It is possible that the Chinese envision economic or political contradictions supplanting the role previously played by military rivalries, but this hardly comports with the normative vision of a world without major conflicts of interest.

In addition, the role of Japan would be transformed profoundly under such hypothetical arrangements. With Tokyo fully incorporated within the US-Japanese alliance framework, Japan has had neither incentives nor opportunities to exercise its power in autonomous fashion. In a world where alliances cease to have relevance, Japan would not encounter comparable inhibitions. Even assuming a resumption of collaborative Sino-American relations congruent with those existing prior to Tiananmen, Chinese leaders would almost certainly describe these changes in strategic terms—that is, they would denote America's need to balance China's political weight against the influence of other major powers. It is, therefore, difficult to discern a regional framework freed from competition or antagonism, although the possibility of such an outcome cannot be excluded.

Case Two: A Soviet Breakthrough in East Asia. The second case assumes a qualitative transformation in the Soviet political-military position in East Asia and in the character of Soviet-US relations within the region. Moscow and Washington would greatly diminish their military competition, and the Soviet Union (or, perhaps more plausibly, the Russian republic) would collaborate far more extensively with the major capitalist powers of East Asia, especially Japan. Moscow's recognition of South Korea is a possible prototype of such a breakthrough, since it demonstrates the Soviet Union's readiness to disengage from political, economic, and security commitments when other opportunities and needs have assumed much greater precedence. The prospect of collaborative Soviet-Japanese ties represents a far larger challenge, since it would require Soviet territorial concessions to Japan as the price for fuller economic integration within the Pacific rim. Although Mikhail Gorbachev's April 1991 trip to Japan seems very unlikely to achieve such a major breakthrough, it at least affords a hypothetical prospect for such an outcome at a future date.

In the second scenario, Moscow would interact principally with the region's capitalist states, not its erstwhile socialist allies or China. Soviet policymakers would not need to choose among China, Japan, and the United States, but the stakes with the latter two would be incalculably larger. Recent Soviet foreign policy collaboration with the United States over Korea and Cambodia, for example, suggests superpower "leapfrogging" of the Asian communist states to reshape the political landscape; it is no accident that steps toward Sino-Vietnamese reconciliation have followed these moves, rather than preceding them.

In theory, Chinese policymakers would welcome a major reduction in the Soviet-US military competition, since it could also reduce US pressures on Japan to enhance its security role, at least as it would affect Northeast Asia. The USSR or a Russian government might then have a far larger and more comprehensive stake in Asia and the Pacific, not one skewed disproportionately to the military sphere. But there remains the real possibility that China might become a peripheral actor in this process, raising yet again the prospect that its political opportunities would diminish rather than increase under a far less antagonistic superpower framework.

Case Three: An Isolated China. The third case assumes that China will be unable to sustain its collaboration with the West or with its neighbors along the Pacific. A much weakened China would display highly antagonistic attitudes toward the outside world. Chinese economic growth and its access to Western markets would diminish, perhaps in the aftermath of an unsuccessful reversion of Hong Kong to PRC sovereignty. With China no longer able to secure predictable access to Western capital and technology, its incentives to collaborate with its capitalist neighbors would diminish, thereby removing inhibitions against threatening its neighbors (perhaps most immediately, Taiwan). China would be compelled to rely on economic and technological linkages to the socialist world and to Third World states; these relations would be born of weakness and necessity, not design. An even worse case for China would entail steady Soviet economic and political integration within the Pacific rim while the Chinese economy lapsed into stagnation or decline.

Under such a nightmare scenario, Chinese and Japanese interests would prove highly antagonistic. As in the 1950s and 1960s, a defiantly nationalistic China would be heavily armed, and would likely find itself embroiled in renewed territorial disputes with its neighbors. Japan would have clear incentives to sustain its defense buildup, and to press the United States to remain militarily engaged in the West Pacific. For both China and Japan, this scenario would be the worst of all possible worlds, but it is not implausible, especially should the legitimacy and viability of the Chinese regime remain under challenge.

Case Four: China as the Regionally Predominant Power. As China increasingly competes for economic assistance from the West with Eastern Europe and the Soviet Union, it may be far less the object of external solicitation than in the past. Beijing's estrangement from the industrial democracies since Tiananmen lends further credence to this picture. China may, therefore, opt to base its policy closer to home, premised on three principal assumptions. First, China's East Asian neighbors (including Japan) have a far more immediate stake in avoiding any long-term estrangement from China than the United States or the European powers. A highly volatile China could have horrendous spillover consequences for the region as a whole that others living in the shadow of China will want to avoid. Second, China's immediate neighbors (especially Hong Kong, Taiwan, and South Korea) increasingly face labor shortages and the need for new markets; China's coastal regions therefore provide a promising avenue for trade and investment. Third, as Confucian cultures, China's neighbors are likely to be far more accepting of highly authoritarian politics, and of the necessity to reassert strong central control. But Taiwan might view ties with China's more dynamic coastal areas as a means of further eroding the power of an already weakened central government.

Beijing, for its part, would seek to utilize fully its cultural and geographic proximity to the world's most rapidly developing region. Chinese strategists may also believe that major regional trading blocs will prove decisive to the global economy of the twenty-first century, especially as European and North American economic integration proceed apace.[19] But the Chinese would also expect a measure of strategic deference from their neighbors. Should the United States and the Soviet Union draw down their military assets presently deployed in East Asia, China by default would become the predominant military power in the region, which only Japan could challenge. Indeed, Chinese strategists may believe that the Soviet Union will opt for a "Europe first" strategy, with Asia and the Pacific more peripheral to Soviet or Russian strategic calculations. If Moscow's destinies remain linked principally to Europe rather than to Asia, it might also ultimately contemplate larger strategic understandings with the Chinese, including a significant role in China's military modernization. The Soviet Union could thus revisit its strategic gamble of the 1950s, but with the prospect of a much more powerful and autonomous China than under the Sino-Soviet alliance.

Japanese responses would prove critical under this scenario. Although Japan has long since left China behind, there remains widespread remorse over Japanese aggression of the 1930s. As Fred Ikle and Terumasa Nakanishi have observed, this historical record lends a "moral coloration" to Sino-Japanese relations precisely opposite to that employed in Soviet-Japanese relations: in the case of China, "Japan's invasion of Manchuria in the 1930s reverses the placement of guilt and grievance."[20] The absence of an overt military rivalry with China has represented a distinct plus for Japan, and Tokyo retains substantial incentives to avoid such a competition in the future.

But Japanese security calculations, including its ability to avoid a military rivalry with China, have always depended on Tokyo's alliance with the United States. Should the US-Japanese relationship prove increasingly unsteady, more worrisome possibilities could also develop. Richard Nixon, for example, has even raised the specter of a Sino-Japanese proto-alliance that would dominate East Asia economically and militarily.[21]

However far-fetched the case may seem, it also suggests the capacity for extraordinary political and strategic realignment in a world no longer constrained by Soviet-US bipolarity.

Case Five: A US-Japan Duopoly. The fifth case assumes growing US-Japanese economic, political, and military domination of Asia and the Pacific. The combined power of the two states, which together account for 40 percent of the world's gross domestic product, would permit them to exercise pervasive influence within the region. If the US political and economic role in Europe were to diminish appreciably, this scenario would assume greater plausibility. In an Asian context, there would be no coalition of countervailing powers that would be able to contest US-Japanese predominance. The Soviets and Chinese seem likely to face prolonged internal preoccupations that make the credible exercise of power beyond their borders much more problematic. The USSR would presumably concentrate its residual strength and energies on Europe, where the stakes for its long-term power position remain incalculably greater. Although Soviet and Chinese incentives for mutual collaboration would increase, neither would constitute major challengers for international influence in East Asia.

There would be inescapable contradictions between Japanese and Chinese power and national ambitions in such a scenario. To the extent that Japan's security contribution to this partnership would be less pronounced than its economic contribution, the dissonance in Sino-Japanese relations could possibly be managed. But China would definitely rank on a lower rung in the region's evolving structure of power, and Sino-US ties would be all but certain to deteriorate.

A more realistic variant of this scenario would entail an expanding US-Japanese partnership, but without the implication of condominium. Conflicts of interest would persist between Tokyo and Washington, but the incentives for interdependence would vastly outweigh issues that divide them. The challenge for Japan would be to articulate and execute a credible political role in the 1990s and beyond commensurate with Japan's economic and technological capabilities, and congruent with emergent challenges to global security.[22] Such a role would emphasize Japanese needs and interests, but still be firmly embedded within a US-Japanese alliance structure. However, Japan's potential role in "out-of-area" conflicts, such as the Persian Gulf, would evoke great suspicions on the part of the Chinese and other regional actors. The challenge would be to integrate national actions in an appropriate multilateral framework. But Japanese activism beyond the economic arena would attest to the qualitative transformation of the US-Japanese relationship. Japan would no longer be hostage to facile arguments about burden-sharing; it would be a global collaborator of the United States, and not consigned to a largely subordinate role in the alliance. Here as well, China's political and strategic significance would pale by comparison.

Case Six: A Fractured US-Japanese Alliance. The sixth case assumes a breakdown in the US-Japanese relationship that has anchored US policy in Asia for the past four decades. As a consequence of mounting domestic resentments and pressures on both sides of the Pacific, perhaps abetted by US dissatisfaction about the scope and character of Japan's contributions in the Persian Gulf, the fabric of US-Japanese relations would unravel, rendering all estimates about East Asia's future highly uncertain. The proximate cause of such a rupture in relations would be the economic tensions that have bedeviled ties since major trade imbalances favoring Japan first developed in the 1970s. But a more profound set of antagonisms seems increasingly evident in both countries. Washington and Tokyo may begin to treat one another as antagonists, although not necessarily in a military sense. But nationalistic resentments would ultimately lead to a breakdown of existing political, security, and institutional arrangements.

In the aftermath of such a rupture, both states would have to recalculate their basic national strategies. It is possible, for example, that the United States would pursue enhanced collaboration with some of Tokyo's neighbors (including China) in order to constrain the exercise of Japanese power. Alternatively, the United States might retreat into an angry unilateralist stance that would seek to avoid "entangling alliances."

In the event of such a worst case, most observers would anticipate a resurgent, highly nationalistic Japan that would seek to exercise dominant political as well as economic influence in East Asia. Freed from the moorings of the US-Japan alliance, Tokyo would no longer be equivocal in its exercise of power. Should Japanese military power develop more fully, this would very likely pose a direct threat to China and other East Asian states. Such an outcome might also entail collusive understandings between Tokyo and Moscow, with the Soviet Union prepared to cede regional predominance to Japan as compensation for the downgrading of the US-Japan relationship, and hence the erosion of American influence in Asia.

A more plausible variant to this scenario would entail a much more conflictive US-Japan relationship, but not an outright rupture in the alliance. But the end result would still be a far less stable relationship, in which elites in both systems would more actively explore alternatives to their present interdependence. The larger questions would remain: Would common interests outweigh contradictions? To what extent would either state be prepared to place the larger relationship at risk for pursuit of more nationalistic goals? Would either country seek coalition partners to caution or inhibit the other's exercise of power?

Under such circumstances, the Chinese might see opportunities as well as dangers. Should Japan's leaders become convinced that the United States was no longer prepared to uphold its security, Japanese strategists would necessarily seek to define a more autonomous strategic concept. Such a step would almost certainly entail a larger military role for Japan, to the consequent detriment of Chinese interests. But a Japan in search of coalition partners might approach China on a different basis, seeking to secure stronger political support from China in exchange for economic and technological inducements. Thus, regardless of their suspicions of Japanese power, leaders in Beijing might perceive opportunities in a more antagonistic Japanese-US relationship, paralleling the leverage Beijing has at times enjoyed between the Soviet Union and the United States.

A Less Predictable Era

East Asia has begun to enter a much less predictable era, with future relations between China and Japan among the larger uncertainties. This relationship will not necessarily become antagonistic, but the inhibitions constraining such a possibility seem much less pronounced than during the past two decades. Although our analysis has operated largely at the level of international structure, the dynamics within both systems may have an equally potent effect, quite possibly reshaping political and strategic patterns in unanticipated ways. Indeed, domestic and institutional forces may prove the ultimate determinants of East Asia's political and strategic future, including the capacity of China, Japan, and other national actors to restrain and to balance their separate political and strategic ambitions. The forecasts in this essay are necessarily conjectural, but they warrant a much more sober judgment on the future prospects for Sino-Japanese relations.

NOTES

1. This paper draws heavily on Jonathan D. Pollack, "The Sino-Japanese Relationship and East Asian Security: Patterns and Implications," *The China Quarterly,* December 1990, pp. 714–29.

2. For an extremely helpful exception, see Takashi Inoguchi, "Four Japanese Scenarios for the Future," *International Affairs,* Winter 1988/89, pp. 15–28.

3. For more detailed discussion, see Jonathan D. Pollack, *The Lessons of Coalition Politics: Sino-American Security Relations* (Santa Monica CA: The RAND Corporation, R-3133-AF, February 1984).

4. On Sino-Japanese military contacts, see Allen S. Whiting, *China Eyes Japan,* (Berkeley and Los Angeles: University of California Press, 1989), pp. 131–34.

5. For my own views, see Pollack, *The Sino-Soviet Summit-Implications for East Asia and U.S. Foreign Policy* (New York: The Asia Society, May 1989).

6. Pei Monong, "On the Trilateral Relationship of the United States, Japan, and ASEAN," *Guoji Wenti Yanjiu,* No. 4, 13 October 1984,

pp. 10–18; trans. in Joint Publications Research Service (JPRS)-CPS-85-006, pp. 1–15.

7. For a relevant example, see Zhu Chun, "Growing Role of the Asian-Pacific Region in the World Strategic Pattern," *International Strategic Studies* (Beijing), No. 2, 1987, pp. 1–10.

8. On Chinese responses to the one-percent decision, see Whiting, *China Eyes Japan,* especially pp. 134–41.

9. See Xi Louren, "An Exploration of the Issue of Japan's March From An 'Economic Power' to a 'Political Power,'" *Guoji Wenti Yanjiu,* No. 4, October 1987, in JPRS-CAR-88-002, pp. 1-4; see also Huan Xiang, "Sino-U.S. Relations Over the Past Year," *Liaowang* (Overseas Edition), 11 January 1988, in *FBIS-China,* 15 January 1988, especially p. 3.

10. Zhao is cited in *Renmin Ribao,* 28 February 1988, p. 1, in *FBIS-China,* 29 February 1988, p. 13.

11. For a report on the Deng-Takeshita exchanges, see *Asahi Shimbun,* 30 August 1988.

12. All citations are from Ge Gengfu, "Changes in the Development of Japan's Defense Policy and Defense Capabilities," *Guoji Wenti Yanjiu,* No. 1, 13 January 1989, in JPRS-CAR-89-032, pp. 6–12.

13. Xi Zhihao, "Japan is Stepping Up Arms Expansion," *Jiefangjun Bao,* 28 August 1989, in *FBIS-China,* 14 September 1989, pp. 5–6.

14. All citations are from Zhao Jieqi, "The Present Status and Prospect of Japan-U.S. Military Relations," *International Strategic Studies* (Beijing), No. 4, 1989, pp. 12–18.

15. All citations are from Zi Jian, "Two Problems in U.S.-Japanese Relations," *Shijie Zhishi,* No. 13, 1 July 1990, in *FBIS-China,* 6 August 1990, pp. 1–2.

16. A "well-informed Chinese official" has disclosed that the PLA has pressed for additional funds in the forthcoming Eighth Five Year Plan to counter Japanese military capabilities. Nicholas D. Kristof, "China, Reassessing its Foes, Views Japan Warily," *The New York Times,* 23 October 1990. Kristof also cites an internal Chinese publication (*Neican Xuanpian*) that deems China a military and economic counterweight to Japan. If confirmed, these disclosures would indicate a major shift in China's future defense planning guidance. These would formalize the reassessment of Japanese power underway since the mid-1980s.

17. For a highly discerning Chinese assessment, see Chen Xiaogong, "World Military Situation in the 1990s," *Jiefangjun Bao,* 7 September 1990, in *FBIS-China,* 27 September 1990, pp. 4–8.

18. See U.S. Department of Defense, Commission on Integrated Long-Term Strategy, *Sources of Change in the Future Security Environment* (Washington: US Government Printing Office, October 1988).

19. Wang Hexing, "The Rise and Impact of Regional Economic Groupings," *Guoji Wenti Yanjiu,* No. 2, 13 April 1990, trans. in JPRS-CAR-90-060, pp. 1–7.

20. Fred Charles Ikle and Terumasa Nakanishi, "Japan's Grand Strategy," *Foreign Affairs,* Summer 1990, p. 84.

21. See Nixon's interview in *Time,* 2 April 1990, p. 49.

22. For a provocative effort to define such a future course, see Ikle and Nakanishi, "Japan's Grand Strategy."

US-JAPANESE ALLIANCE IN THE CHANGING WORLD

Ambassador Hisahiko Okazaki

Ambassador Hisahiko Okazaki joined the Ministry of Foreign Affairs after receiving his law degree from Tokyo University. He subsequently received an M.A. degree from Cambridge University. He has been a visiting fellow at CSIS, Georgetown University, and at the RAND corporation, and a visiting scholar at Harvard University. In his diplomatic career he has served as First Secretary, the Embassy of Japan, Washington, DC, and as ambassador to Saudi Arabia and to Thailand, his current post. Ambassador Okazaki has also been director-general of the Research and Planning Department of the Ministry of Foreign Affairs. He is the author of several books including **A Grand Strategy for Japan's Security** and **Mutsu Munemitsu.**

It is undeniable that a fundamental change is taking place in world politics. We must, of course, be cautious when we consider the future development of the revolution which is taking place in Eastern Europe and the Soviet Union. It is still undetermined whether conservatives or reformists will win in the Soviet Union, or whether the present reforms will fragment the Soviet empire, or, as the word *"perestroika"* originally was intended to convey, revitalize it. Nonetheless, it is a matter of fact that the Warsaw Treaty organization has disintegrated, and cannot be re-established in the foreseeable future. This has created a large buffer zone between the NATO countries and the Soviet Union, and drastically lengthened the warning time for any contingency, even if the Soviet Union emerges as a newly revitalized power.

Thus, Western Europe is now enjoying a period in which threats from outside are at their lowest for the last half century, and looking towards a new world order. The question now posed, repeatedly, is whether a parallel development will take place in Asia, and if so, when this will happen.

The difference between Asia and Europe has already been the subject of much discussion among experts in Asian affairs. Whilst Europe has, essentially, been characterized by the confrontation between the clearly separated blocs of NATO and the Wasaw Pact, in Asia each region has its own particular problems, especially those of divided countries. While the European military balance of power is determined by the quality and quantity of ground forces on each side, the US naval presence carries a substantial weight in the Western Pacific and the immediately surrounding regions. Because of the number of individual problems, the solution of each being of greatest immediate importance to the protagonists, a comprehensive détente or disarmament is impractical in Asia.

All the above arguments are correct in themselves. In a sense, however, a parallel development has taken place in Asia, beginning even earlier than in Europe. It appears that the Soviet Union started to curtail its global overextension in the mid-1980s. The change in Eastern Europe was dramatic, mainly due to the fact that the Eastern European nations, with the exception of Yugoslavia and Albania, were forced to become Communist states by Soviet military intervention, and since the Soviet Union decided to reduce its overextension, the Communist regime collapsed immediately. In Southeast Asia, the Soviet Union has decided to discontinue grant assistance to Vietnam and, subsequently, the Hun Sen regime in Cambodia, and is, in addition, partially withdrawing its forces from Cam Ranh Bay. If Vietnam had been a state similar to Czechoslovakia or Hungary, internal political changes would have been equally dramatic. Since Vietnam, however, is a state which, like China, has achieved independence by internal revolution with its own forces, the Soviet withdrawal did not produce the same effect.

The Soviet Union apparently decided on a radical change of strategy in the mid-1980s. In Asia, this change can be perceived in the Vladivostok speech of Gorbachov in 1986, with the declaration of withdrawal from Afghanistan, and the resumption of talks with China regarding borders. The symptoms are also conspicuous in Russian military behaviour. The naval exercise held in 1984 was the last to have global strategic implications. After that year, Russian naval exercises in the Pacific seem to be more concentrated on the defence of the Okhotsk Sea and the northern Sea of Japan. This observation can be supported by the number of passages made by warships through the three straits around Japan; the number of passages through the Soya Strait increased steadily all through the 1980s, whilst those through the Tsugaru and Tsushima straits remained constant or even decreased slightly after 1985. This could well indicate that the Soviet Union has changed its strategy, curtailing overextension in Afghanistan, in Vietnam, and on the Sino-Soviet border, and concentrating on the defense of the Pacific Coast of the Russian Republic.

Since the end of the 1970s, the Okhotsk Sea and the northern part of the Sea of Japan have become increasingly important in Soviet strategy. With the introduction of long-range sea-launched ballistic missiles those areas became a most desirable sea bastion for the second strike strategic nuclear capability. It is understandable that the Soviet Union, whilst curtailing its

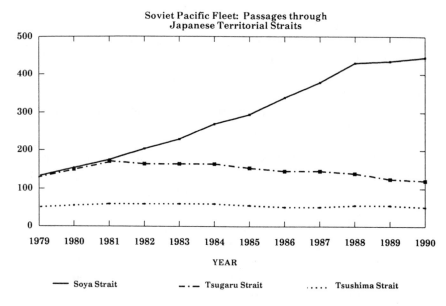

Soviet Pacific Fleet: Passages through
Japanese Territorial Straits

——— Soya Strait   — · — Tsugaru Strait   . . . . . Tsushima Strait

Table 1

Year	Tsushima Strait	Tsugaru Strait	Soya Strait
1979	140	50	130
1980	150	55	155
1980	170	60	175
1982	165	60	205
1983	165	60	230
1984	165	60	270
1985	155	55	295
1986	145	50	340
1987	145	50	380
1988	140	55	430
1989	125	55	435
1990	120	50	445

Source: JDA, <u>Defense of Japan</u>
Produced by Lt. Col. S. NISHIMURA

overextension all over the world, including Eastern Europe, is concentrating its available resources on preserving its last and most prized deterrent capability against the United States. Of the two sea bastions of the Barentz Sea and the Okhotsk Sea, the latter is the more desirable, as it is surrounded by a chain of islands, whilst the former is open to the Arctic Ocean and more vulnerable to the US attack submarines.

This development has resulted in Southeast Asia enjoying a halcyon period with minimum threat from outside the region. The threat of colonial imperialism, so prevalent in previous centuries, is already past. The Japanese military advance was short-lived. During the long Cold War period the region was subject to Communist threats, which culminated, internally, in Indonesia with the 30 September 1965 incident, and externally with the invasion of Cambodia by Vietnamese Forces and Soviet advances in Cam Ranh Bay. The Communist threat to the region now seems to have receded, due to the Soviet withdrawal. The normalisation of relations with China by both Indonesia and Singapore indicates that those countries no longer fear internal Communist insurgency sponsored by China. The potential and historical threat of China always remains, and the Indian naval build-up is watched with concern, but these threats are still far away on the horizon. The so-called "revival" of Japanese militarism lacks reality in the sense that a Japanese military initiative is inconceivable under present international circumstances.

Thus, Southeast Asia is enjoying the best period in its history, combined with the prospect of the fastest economic growth in the world. Indeed, its present state of affairs may well be considered to be better than that of Europe. It is for this reason, amongst others, that ASEAN nations are reluctant to subscribe to the idea of a "New World Order" approach canvassed by either the Soviet Union, or Australia and other nations. The ASEAN nations say "We are quite well off at present, without any particular new arrangement. Why should we have to have one?"

This new world trend places Japan in a unique position. First of all, Japan remains as practically the sole area where the potential Soviet military threat has not diminished. Indeed, it may even have increased. Even Finland, which has always been under threat from Russia, has a partial buffer zone in the Baltic States. Similarly Turkey, which has for more than a century been under Russian pressure, now has the Caucasian states as a buffer zone. Iran has gained much the same advantages due to developments in Azerbaijan and Central Asia. China has, at least temporarily, settled its border questions.

In the case of Japan, the area immediately adjacent to Japan has become the only area of increased military concentration by the Soviet Union. The Maritime Province had been the hinterland of the Koreans, but they were forcibly evacuated to Central Asia during Stalin's rule, and all Japanese people were expelled from Sakhalin and the Kurils. The Maritime Province is now, therefore, a fully homogeneous and integral part of the Russian Republic, and is in no way a buffer zone.

Secondly, territorial issues still exist between Japan and the Soviet Union. Since the Helsinki agreement (CSCE) in 1975, the Soviet Union has persistently advised Japan to accept a parallel arrangement, which Japan, in turn, has consistently refused. The Helsinki agreement is based on the recognition of the de facto borders which have existed since the end of World War II. This was the greatest concession made by the West during the so called "First Détente" period. The agreement was possible for two principal reasons. First, the nations which lost part of their territories (East Germany, Poland, Czechoslovakia, and Romania) were in no position to raise objections with the Soviet Union at that time. Second, the Western nations, (the United States, Great Britain, and France) stood to lose nothing from their own territories and, perhaps, did not foresee a situation where even the legitimacy of the annexation of the Baltic states would come into question. Japan, however, lost part of its own proper territory by Soviet military occupation, and Japan is not a country which has to obey the Soviet Union.

CSCE is the cause, rather than the result, of the collapse of the Soviet empire, even though it is now regarded as the instrument for the new world order as mooted in the Paris conference. In the Malta talks, practically the only aim of Gorbachev was to get reassurance from President Bush that the United

States would observe the obligations of the Helsinki agreement. Without this assurance in respect of existing borders, Gorbachev could not possibly have shed his empire in Eastern Europe.

Japan's position can thus be seen as unique in world history. Even though this is not the fault of Japan, when everyone else speaks of a "New World Order,""Détente," and "Global disarmament," Japan is placed in an awkward position. This situation is not new. Historically, Japan's position has always been unique because of geographical and historical conditions.

In order to find out where we are and where we should go from here it is important to discern what the long-term Japanese and US policy goals are, respectively, in world affairs. At this time of historical change we have to look back into history and geopolitics. Fortunately, the diplomatic histories and experience of both Japan and the United States are not very long, starting virtually from the middle of the 19th century in this region. During the intervening years, goestrategy has not changed much.

Japanese Geopolitics

Russian threat. Since the modern Western powers reached the furthest Eastern part of the Eurasian continent in the 18th century, Russia has constantly been the greatest threat to Japan's security. In that sense, Japan's experience with Russia is somewhat similar to that of Finland, Poland, Turkey, Persia, and China, and quite different from that of Western Europe and the North American nations.

As long ago as 1806, Lieutenant Khvostov attacked the Japanese settlement in Sakhalin Island. The Russian threat became increasingly potent as Russia occupied the Amur River estuary and its adjacent territory in 1860, and constructed the Siberian railroad which was completed in 1902. Russia has always been a threat to Japan's security whether it was Tzarist or Communist. In this sense, changes of Russian polity, or the ideology on which it is based, have little effect on Japan's security circumstances, although a period of revolution would usually give Japan a breathing space.

Japanese military capability has never been superior to that of Russia. Although Japan won the Russo-Japanese War (1904–5), it was a victory against the local Russian army in the Far East. At the time they concluded a peace treaty, the Russian army, reinforced from Europe, had a definite numerical superiority over the Japanese army. Had not the Tzar accepted the peace treaty because of a naval defeat and revolutions within Russia, the destiny of the Japanese army in Manchuria and Korea would have been the same as that of Napoleon in Moscow. Even at the height of Japanese military power in the 1930s, the Japanese army had not planned on reaching Irkutsk and was incapable of occupying Vladivostok, whereas the Soviet Union always had the potential to defeat the Japanese army anywhere on the continent.

Alliance with hegemonic powers. The only way to assure Japan's security in the face of this formidable Russian empire was for Japan to ally itself with the then world hegemonic powers, Great Britain or the United States. These hegemonic powers claimed superiority over the seven seas and could, therefore, assure the security of an island nation like Japan as well as free access to resources by trading with every corner of the world.

During the 20 years of Anglo-Japanese alliance and the 40 years of the US-Japanese alliance the Japanese people have been completely confident of their own security and have enjoyed freedom and democracy. Some people believe that Japan's democracy was installed by the Americans during the post-World War II occupation. Bismark once said, "A fool learns from his own experience, but I learn from history". For our generation, the memory of the last war was so formidable that very few would go back to earlier history. They remember only the prewar militaristic period in Japan and try to find the fundamental identity of the Japanese nation in that period. Japanese democracy, however, has a deep tradition going back to the opening of its gates to Western civilization in 1853. Since that time, there was a continuous struggle by popular movements toward parliamentary democracy for 40 years, and a British-style democracy, called the "Taisho" democracy, flourished during the first 20 years of the 20th century. When the Americans occupied Japan in 1945, Japan specialists, above all Dr. Edwin Reischauer, advised the occupation authorities to revive Taisho democracy. This advice was accepted and even now Japan's electoral system is almost identical with that prevailing at the end of Taisho period.

Wrong choice between alternatives. After that, Japan entered a period in which it lost sight of the Russian threat. In the wake of the Russian Revolution, Russian influence in the Far East had been significantly reduced. Northern Manchuria, which had been under Russian influence even after Russia's defeat in the Russo-Japanese War, was abandoned. The Far Eastern part of Russia did not come under the control of the Communist central government until some time after the revolution. Meanwhile, the rise of the Third Reich threatened the security of the Soviet Union and attracted Soviet attention to the European front.

In this period, Japan forgot about the potential threat of the Soviet Union and the vital importance of alliance with the Anglo-American world. Thus it was that Japan started an adventure on the Asian continent which was destined to bring about confrontation with not only the Soviet Union but also the Anglo-American world. This proved to be a fatal mistake.

The Japanese are not a special race; Japanese people want first, security, then prosperity, and freedom. Democracy flourished during the Anglo-Japanese alliance. After its lapse the Japanese people felt insecure. The security concerns of the nation in this period overrode the desire for freedom and democracy. Soldiers seemed more reliable than politicians. Soldiers concentrate on security absolutely; they are not satisfied with 100 percent security and look for 120 percent. Japan's minimum *lebensraum* was traditionally the southern part of Korea but it was now extended to Manchuria. The history of this period demonstrates the indivisible relationship between Japan's security environment and its democracy and the ratio that led to the wrong choice being made.

American Interest

The Russian Policy of the United States. For the United States the Soviet Union remains the only power which can threaten its security. This will continue to be so in the foreseeable future, and it is inevitable since the United States has succeeded to Great Britain's role of hegemonic power. In Europe there have been several traditional ways of dealing with Russia. Great Britain often used the diplomacy of balance of power and was quite often even allied with Russia.

In the Far East, however, the options are rather limited. At the turn of the century, Great Britain boasted of its "splendid isolation" but had no choice but to enter into an Anglo-Japanese alliance in the Far East to counter the Russian advance toward the Pacific and China. This is the best example of Japan's unique geostrategic position. When the Anglo-American world recognises the potential threat of Russia as its only adversary in global politics, the best alternative is to have an alliance with Japan. In fact, the 20 years of Anglo-Japanese alliance and 40 years of US-Japanese alliance were periods when the interests of the Anglo-American world in the Asia-Pacific-Indian Ocean area were best guaranteed. In this sense, the long-term interests of Japan and the United States nearly converge.

The United States also had a period during which it lost sight of the potential Russian threat. In the 1930s and 1940s, after the lapse of the Anglo-Japanese alliance, the Japanese threat certainly must have looked bigger than that of the Soviet Union. It was pointed out, however, even by American experts, that it would be dangerous to lose sight of the Soviet threat by destroying Japan's influence in the Far East. Another reason for the United States to have lost sight of the Russian threat was sentimental preoccupation with China and, consequently, animosity towards Japan.

China policy of the United States. Theoretically speaking, American diplomacy has other choices. The United States could go back to isolationism and withdraw from Asia. This is an unrealistic proposal so long as the United States is a hegemonic power. The United States could manage Asian affairs under a condominium with the Soviet Union. This option is also unrealistic as long as the Soviet Union is the greatest potential adversary of the United States. China could serve as another American choice. During the Second World War one of the American war aims was to replace Japan with China as a potential key to the stability of Asia. This idea was, however, frustrated by the fact that China became Communist. A similar possibility has not been floated recently; instead there are suggestions to explore the possibility of a European-style balance of power between Japan and China.

It is an unresolved question whether China could be a partner in an alliance in the traditional sense. China has never been in alliance with other countries in the classic way of 19th century power politics. China is an empire in itself. The greatest difference between Japan and China is that China is not afraid of isolation. China has an unparallelled strategic defense capability because of its large territory and population. Therefore, its diplomacy is always independent. Outside nations cannot influence its foreign policy either by military threat or by the contractual obligations of an alliance. The most orthodox way to deal with China is to respect its independence and sovereignty and adjust the national interest of the United States and China, case by case, depending on then-existing international circumstances.

Compared with China, Japan is a nation which is over-populated, poorly endowed with natural resources, and therefore fragile in its economic dependence on overseas resources. Its people are extremely well educated, very fast to absorb information from abroad and nervous in reacting to this information.

An alliance should have a potential adversary and should have mutual military obligations. This is the only orthodox way to ensure a sense of security to the people of contracting nations. The League of Nations, established after the Versailles Peace Treaty, did not serve to bring a sense of security to European nations. The so-called 9 Power Treaty after the abolition of the Anglo-Japanese alliance, gave a feeling of insecurity to the Japanese people and prompted them to support an independent defense policy and the enlargement of Japanese *lebensraum* on the Asian continent.

If the security side of the US-Japan alliance were to be toned down, people would quickly perceive its security implication and start to explore a new policy direction. American-style politics in post-war Japan would accelerate an erratic shift of public mood and make the future course of Japanese politics fluid. Therefore, for the purpose of securing stability in the Asia-Pacific region, it is desirable to maintain the US-Japan military alliance, while clearly recognising the potential threat of the Soviet Union.

Preserving the democracy of Japan should be one of the US policy goals in the Far East. It sounds like an egotistical argument for Japan to say that the US-Japanese alliance is necessary for safeguarding Japan's democracy. However, it is also desirable for the United States to have a solid alliance with a stable democratic country, such as Japan, in the Far East. American interests are best served by maintaining a solid alliance with Japan, friendly relations with China, and by constantly adjusting mutual national interests between all parties.

Joint efforts to maintain the alliance. The current inclination, however, is a definite drift toward underplaying the military necessity of the alliance in the prevailing mood of détente. Therefore, the policy of maintaining the solid military alliance has to face considerable difficulties in the domestic politics of both the United States and Japan. In order to survive this difficult period and consolidate the US-Japanese alliance, both governments have to endeavour to persuade their countrymen of the importance of the alliance by means of good publicity. To make the alliance truly beneficial to each partner, a fundamental restructuring is in order.

It is not really difficult to persuade the Japanese people of the wisdom of continuing the alliance. Of course, the left-wing will renew its arguments against the alliance now that the perception of the Soviet threat is drastically reduced by détente. However, the left wing can suggest no constructive alternative. Formerly, their alternative was a partnership with the Soviet Union and China, but their credibility has now dropped further than their threats. One of the most forceful arguments against the alliance in the past was that the US-Japan alliance would involve Japan in a war which Japan would not like; that is, a war between the United States and the Soviet Union. This argument has lost its impact as the possibility of war has become remote. The majority of Japanese people, particularly in business circles, are securely ensconced in the concept of the US-Japan alliance and they are very happy to see the alliance continue.

The real problem is: How can Japan satisfy the American people? In the past 40 years Americans have voiced some dissatisfaction regarding the conduct of Japan as an ally; the United States has always wanted to see Japan spending more of its budget on the defense effort and becoming involved in US operations outside Japan. Thus, the United States has deplored some Japanese domestic constraints which have prevented Japan from cooperating with the United States in the military field. Particularly in recent years, the United States has sought a partnership with Japan, with its immense resources, to help the United States fulfill its global responsibilities and has complained about Japan's uncooperative attitude. In spite of all these complaints the United States has accepted a compromise with Japan, mainly because of Japan's tremendous strategic importance, which the United States could not possibly do without in the period of severe East-West confrontation. The potential threat of the Soviet Union still exists but the perception of it is diminishing—it is not sufficient to convince the American people and Congress of the urgent need to continue the alliance. We need a comprehensive new theory to justify the necessity for the alliance.

- The first purpose of the US-Japan alliance should obviously be to build up and maintain a stable military balance against the Soviet military capability in the Western Pacific. This is important not only for Japan and Korea but also for the security and stability of the entire Asian-Pacific region. The only period (1979–1985) in which the balance became unstable was precisely the time when Southeast Asia was exposed to the Soviet threat for the first time in history.

- The second US purpose in the alliance is to utilize Japan, which is their most stable ally in Asia, as an intermediary point of transportation and communication for the entire region of the Pacific and Indian Oceans.

- Third, the United States has borne enormous military expenditure in the past 40 years and is now suffering from a budget deficit. The United States would like to take advantage of the flourishing economy of Japan to maximize its share of the financial burden.

Measures to be taken. For the United States, the remaining threat from the Soviet Union is reduced to little else but the strategic nuclear capability. The second strike capabilities are, for the Soviet Union, the ultimate assurance of nuclear deterrence. This circumstance is not likely to change in the forseeable future. It is unrealistic at present to visualise a world in which the Soviet Union considers even the second strike nuclear deterrent unnecessary. Hokkaido has a special geographical significance, as its northeastern coast is the only land foreign to the Soviet Union on the Okhotsk Sea. Hokkaido dominates two straits through which the Soviet fleet, protecting the sea-launched ballistic missiles in the Okhotsk Sea, must pass, since the Mamiya Strait is too shallow to afford passage. Hokkaido has been the territory most coveted by Russia for the last 200 years, and the defense of Hokkaido is, therefore, a vital common concern of both the United States and Japan. The interests of the two countries coincide so long as the Soviet Union remains the only country which can seriously threaten US security, and Japan is not willing to cede sovereignty. It follows, therefore, that the strategy of Japan, the United States, and the US-Japanese alliance should be to maintain a sufficient military presence in Northeast Asia, and to create security and stability in the region around Hokkaido. Although this is a minimum requirement, it will not be an easy task to achieve.

It is an established Soviet strategy to compensate for inferior quality with quantity, and then catch up with quality about a decade later. The Soviet Union succeeded in catching up with the technology of the American 4th Generation aircraft at the end of its great arms build-up from 1965 to 1980. As a result, the Soviet Union set up and started to operate production lines by the middle of the 1980s. This explains why Soviet military modernization continued to accelerate after the Soviet Union as a whole shifted its resources from military production to various *perestroika* measures. If we compare the numbers of fourth generation aircraft available in the region—F–15, F–16, and F–18 on the US and Japanese side, and MiG–29, MiG–31, and SU27 on the Soviet side—Soviet numbers have already surpassed those of the US-Japanese joint forces. This occurred last year, as the diagram on the following page shows.

Soviet forces are expected to grow further in the coming year whilst US forces remain constant. An increase in Japanese forces may cover part of this gap, but not all. The remaining difference could be taken care of today by the modern weapons of the US 7th Fleet and other advanced technology, but it is evident that the gap is widening. The necessary military countermeasure is obvious: an improvement in the quality and quantity of joint Japanese-US defense capabilities.

The required level of combat capabilities is always a function of whatever Soviet capabilities are at the time. *Close consultation will be necessary on the desirable size of the US-Japan joint forces.* It is quite likely that, in view of the existing financial conditions of both countries, the United States could reduce the level of its forces if Soviet capabilities are reduced and Japan may be requested to increase its defense capabilities when those of the Soviets increase. It is understood, however, that the United States would not reduce its combat capabilities in the Far East in the existing military situation. This is a desirable posture in the long term. An essential element in any alliance is the determination of the contracting parties to be prepared to fight shoulder to shoulder on the same front. The maintenance of substantial US combat forces in Japan will provide the stiffening of mutual confidence in the alliance.

An increase in Japanese burden-sharing will concentrate on rear support, at least in the mid-term, while an increase in host nation support will alleviate some of the US financial burden. It is my conviction that, in the long term, it is desirable to increase Japan's support, including logistics and intelligence, in order to limit the American burden of providing frontal combat capabilities. Ideally, as soon as US combat forces come within a range of 1,000 miles of Japan, they could rely on the support of Japan for escort, supplies of fuel, ammunition, and provisions, and also military intelligence in Northeast Asia.

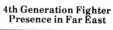

4th Generation Fighter
Presence in Far East

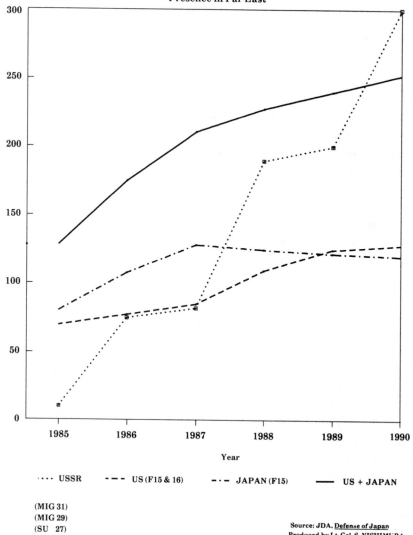

Year

```
···· USSR      - - - US (F15 & 16)      - · - JAPAN (F15)      ⎯⎯ US + JAPAN
```

(MIG 31)
(MIG 29)
(SU 27)

Source: JDA, <u>Defense of Japan</u>
Produced by Lt. Col. S. NISHIMURA

Such an increase in rear support by Japan will facilitate US actions in other Pacific-Indian Ocean areas.

In order to consolidate victory in the Cold War, the United States and Japan should, in the long-term, cooperate in maintaining sufficient superiority in military technology over the Soviet Union. It appears that by the mid-eighties the Soviet Union had caught up with the technological level of most of the American military hardware as the result of the last military industrial surge before *perestroika*. Relying, as always, on quantitative superiority to offset qualitative inferiority the Soviets now claim superiority in numbers of weapons. As time passes, the Soviet Union may regain overall superiority by gradually replacing old weapons with state-of-the-art models developed in the mid-1980s.

One of the main factors which made the Soviet Union propose a truce in the arms race against the United States was SDI. Whether SDI really works or not, the Soviet Union did not have sufficient financial and technological resources to counter it. In Reykjavik Gorbachev is reported to have asked Reagan whether America's intention was to make the Soviet Union bankrupt. If the United States continues to develop and deploy the newest types of weapons in all fields there is a good possibility that the Soviet Union may finally cease its efforts to catch up with America's capabilities. In such a case, America's victory will finally be consolidated. Thus, it is desirable that the United States and Japan, both of which possess the world's highest technological potential, should not slacken their efforts to advance technologically in close cooperation with each other.

Finally, we have to address the new issues of Japan's cooperation in international efforts to maintain world order and peace, particularly in connection with the current Gulf crisis. This issue is primarily a Japanese domestic matter, and has two aspects, one minor and the other major. It is a minor issue to co-operate with the so-called UN peacekeeping operation and to set up Nordic-type standby forces for that purpose. The legal question has long been solved, and now the Japanese public has reached a consensus that a cash check alone will not suffice as Japan's contribution to international cooperation.

The question which remains is, rather, financial and organizational. This is a nice thing, and does not invite any external or internal criticism; it may even contribute to the maintenance of international order in a less stringent case, such as the supervision of future Cambodian elections. It is, however, more in the nature of a political gesture than an exercise of real impact on international politics. In consequence, it is only a partial response to the desire of the United States for increased Japanese cooperation. Moreover, there are limitations to Japan's response in the sense that it works only when the United Nations so decides. This means that, in the event of any serious conflicts of interest between the United States and another major power, Japan is unable to cooperate with the United States.

The major question is how Japan might share the burden the United States carries in fulfilling its global responsibilities as a loyal partner in the alliance. In the recent crisis, the real issue is hidden behind the Security Council Resolutions. According to American perceptions, however, the real issue is that Japan should have been amongst the first nations to have dispatched troops to Saudi Arabia, with or without the UN Resolutions, considering Japan's vital reliance on oil from the Persian Gulf. On this major issue there is not much to be said at present. Even the bill with the modest purpose of sending the lightly armed Self Defense Force for noncombatant purposes to the Gulf failed to pass in the Diet. In the prevailing domestic situation in Japan, a situation in which Japan could cooperate with US global efforts to an extent which would satisfy America is still a dream.

Meantime, Japan should continue its endeavours to further the cooperation and to consolidate the alliance. Americans, meanwhile, must try to understand that, although full partnership with Japan is the most desirable form of cooperation, Japan is at least performing its minimum—but by far the most important duty for the alliance—in maintaining the military balance in the Northwest Pacific.

US-JAPANESE SECURITY COOPERATION IN THE NEW INTERNATIONAL ORDER

Dr. John E. Endicott

Dr. John E. Endicott, *a former USAF officer and director of the Institute for National Strategic Studies at the National Defense University, is now Professor, International Affairs and Director of the Center for the Study of Strategic and International Issues at the Georgia Institute of Technology. He holds a B.S. from Ohio State University, an M.A. from Omaha University, and M.A., M.A.L.D., and Ph.D. degrees from Tufts University. Dr. Endicott's areas of speciality lie in Asian studies, defense and system stability. He has authored, co-authored, and co-edited* **Japan's Nuclear Option, The Politics of East Asia,** *and the 4th edition of* **American Defense Policy.** *His most recent articles include "Japan's Quiet New International Activism," and "Japanese Security Policy: Stability in an Era of Change?"*

The world has become so accustomed to rapid political change that Japanese participation in a NATO-sponsored conference on "Global Security: North American, European, and Japanese Inter-dependence in the 1990s," went almost unnoticed.[1] Held at Knokke-Heist, a small seaside resort in Belgium, in June 1990, this two-day conference with a Japanese delegation headed by Deputy Foreign Minister Hisashi Owada, was the first instance of participation by an official Japanese delegation in a discussion of security questions outside the narrow confines of the US-Japanese Security Treaty context. It was clearly the first time Japan had sat down with European states to discuss security roles of a more general nature. Little did we, the participants, realize that this initial willingness of the Japanese government to involve itself in a new international security relationship would be put to the test so rapidly.

Since 17 June Japan and the Japanese have engaged in one of the most exhaustive reexaminations of their attitudes toward defense, the Self-Defense Forces, Japan's role in Northeast Asia, the US-Japanese security relationship, and Japan's overall participation in the emerging international order. The debate became keen as the next Mid-Term Defense Plan (*Jikibo*) for the period 1991–1995 was being considered both inside and outside government amid a changing international security environment that was challenging many of the comfortable assumptions that had become key basic planning factors.

These changes involved the dynamics of Soviet policy—both domestic and external—changes in the People's Republic of China that had occurred since 4 June 1989, political reform and diplomatic success for South Korea, and a growing willingness of North Korea to better position itself for its inevitable leadership transition. Not the least of the elements of this fast-moving horizon was the increasing degree of irritation on the part of some actors in the American policy community with the insensitivities of some Japanese counterparts with regard to macro-economic and trading issues that were taking on security implications. (To be sure, this latter feature was a reciprocal relationship.)

Two dates had particular impact on Japan and its internal debate: 2 August 1990, and 17 January 1991. Before 2 August and Iraq's invasion of Kuwait, the debate on the future of US-Japanese security relations took place certainly in a new environment—post-Cold War—but continued to be theoretical and somewhat detached. However, there was one interesting feature; there was some evident searching for a "new relationship." In fact, a considerable number of Japanese commentators called for a new or revised security relationship with America.[2]

Surprisingly, individuals who were long supporters of the US relationship were calling for a major reassessment in light of a lessening Soviet threat and growing economic friction with the United States that increasingly spilled over into the security arena. Some observers were still smarting from the FSX disagreements that seemed to reverse previous decades of close technological cooperation with the United States.[3]

In the early spring of 1990, the Budget Committee of the Lower House of the Diet began two days of deliberations concentrating on defense and foreign policies and the Structural Impediments Initiative Talks. Members of the opposition parties sought to gain commitments from the government to set limits on defense expenditures on an annual basis—rather than a five-year basis as is the practice—and to freeze defense spending in light of the "peace-is-breaking-out " argument that was becoming almost universal. They also called for a review of the 1976 National Defense Program Outline, or *Taiko,* which still served as one of the principal planning documents in light of the reduced threat from the "reformed " Soviet Union.

Prime Minister Toshiki Kaifu, while not agreeing with the proposition, did call for the Japan Defense Force to "modestly increase its defense capabilities . . . " [4] He, in essence, called for Japan to continue its build-up and modernization even though significant changes seemed to be happening to the international system. These were also the ideas and policy line reflected at Knokke-Heist by the Japanese participants. An era of increasing interdependency was discussed where all states would play roles within their own capabilities to ensure the safe transition to a new international order.

Minister Owada stressed the importance of the concept of *pax consortis,* or the "maintenance of order through a mechanism of management based on consultation among the major players of the system."5 Interestingly, the Owada thesis envisaged a system where

> ...no single participant is strong enough to make the system function properly, while each single participant is strong enough to sabotage the system simply by non-cooperation. In this sense it is a highly fragile system, which requires a constant nurturing and strengthening through positive cooperation based on consultation.6

Minister Owada saw Japan playing a "much more positive and constructive role" in the non-military fields of international system stability, especially in East Asia. His opinion was seconded by the other Japanese participants who represented a band of opinion generally supportive of the government position. The important thing, however, was not that those individuals who appeared at the conference happened to agree, it was the overall willingness to accept the concept of a more involved Japan, taking its initial steps onto the world stage as a responsible actor. Even though these initial steps were hedged and focused on economic involvement, it was an indication of two important points: Japan was willing to continue its partnership with the United States in non-military support to the new international order; and Japan did not wish to threaten any of her neighbors by embarking on a program that would militarize her foreign policy.

These points and others were reflected in the lively discussion of the draft five-year defense plan known in Japanese as the *Jikibo* . It was released in June 1990. While continuing the defense increase did seem to fly in the face of the popular notion that peace was breaking out, the Defense Agency justified the build-up with two principal arguments:

—Arms control and reduction talks are not yet in progress in the Asian region, and there are possibilities of instability in the region.

—Japan does not need to review its defense policy, because its buildup goal as set by the 1976 National Defense Program Outline is for attaining minimum defense forces.[7]

This rather "hard line" position on the need to maintain the five-year plan continued until the middle of July when, in the face of news of the Soviet agreement for a unified Germany, the then head of the Defense Agency, Yozo Ishikawa, noted that a somewhat restrained defense budget might be in order. He said: "It is natural . . . to try as much as possible to restrain the scale of the defense budget" in light of easing tensions in Eastern Europe.

As August approached it was clear that Japan had sent several signals to America that it was prepared to play a continuing significant role in its own defense and the US-Japanese Security Treaty relationship; that it desired to reduce economic and trade friction through the conclusion of the Structural Impediments Initiative Talks; and that it was somewhat ready to play a larger—more universal—role in the creation of a new international system to replace that which existed for most of the Cold War. The US-Japanese relationship admittedly was under review from many sources, but it appeared that once these reviews were accomplished, the fundamental importance of the United States to Japan was consistently reaffirmed by the government, the Liberal Democratic Party, and the business community.[8] Concepts for the new international order would be rationally and cautiously advanced, allowing the Japanese political system to fully integrate them—all in good time.

August 1990 to January 1991

On 28 July, approval of the fiscal 1991 budget request was announced. Defense spending received a 5.8 percent increase—the lowest spending increase for defense since fiscal 1961. While peace had not completely broken out, the same pressures that had led responsible US Congressmen to talk in terms of drastic cuts in the defense budget and as few as 100,000 troops in Europe had forced the Defense Agency to make some adjustments in previously announced goals. Advanced hardware such as the AWACS and the multiple rocket-launching system (MLRS) were announced as postponed or cancelled. Even the five-year term for the next build-up plan was being questioned as too long in such a peaceful environment. However, on 2 August, when Iraq invaded Kuwait, Japan came of age as a major actor of the international security community. Discussion of defense and security issues took on a significance unknown to most of the actors.

The story of the next six weeks is a story of both incredible accomplishments and disappointments. Perhaps, in the midst of debate and argument over the Japanese response to the Iraqi action, no specific realization of the impact on the new international system was made, but from 2 August onward, the actions of Japan were clearly the actions of a partner of the United States, and the actions of a state establishing its own precedents with respect to the future. In fact, the story of the next six weeks—until the middle of September—is one that can only be described in "watershed" analogy terms. The reader should recall that it took six years for the Japanese to ratify the Nonproliferation Treaty,[9] and the achievements and failures to be discussed below took less than six weeks.

The "dramatic" pace of decisionmaking during this phase of the crisis in the Persian Gulf stands in powerful contradistinction to claims by the revisionist school that Japan lacks a leadership capable of making rapid decisions. In this sense, the Japanese demonstrated that the system not only works, but that their participation as responsible members of the new international order could take place in fields not necessarily of a military nature. (It was also interesting to observe the constitutional system put to the test during this six-week period.) Prime Minister Toshiki Kaifu proposed a Japanese presence in the Persian Gulf which would have included some form of participation by the Self-Defense Forces. Facing a deadline of 12 November—the enthronement ceremony of the new emperor—and realizing he was not delivering consensus even within the Lower House of the Diet, Kaifu stepped back. Perhaps we would have preferred a different conclusion, but no one can say that the system did not work. Only those who do not appreciate the true nature of participatory democracy and what it means to Japan were heard from.

The Japanese Response

Significantly, on 3 August, only one day after the invasion, Japan condemned the aggression of Iraq, and two days later announced complete economic sanctions against Iraq placing at risk some four billion dollars in Japanese investments. These actions were followed on 6 August with Japanese support for the United Nations Security Council resolution calling for an international trade embargo against Iraq. (For a state without a decisionmaking system, some impressive accomplishments.)

As it became clear that it was America's intention to respond to the Iraqi challenge with a significant military build-up, Prime Minister Kaifu (against his own wishes) gave up a planned trip to Saudi Arabia, Oman, Jordan, Egypt, and Turkey to better coordinate the domestic politics of the Japanese response. Foreign Minister Taro Nakayama was sent in Kaifu's place and the trip that lasted from 17–25 August was billed as a "fact finding" visit.[10]

The Japanese people—much like their US counterparts—were bombarded with information about the crisis. It was announced: that US Marines on Okinawa would be shifted to the Persian Gulf, along with AWACS that had been stationed at Kadena Air Base on Naha; that Japanese citizens could not leave Iraq; and that Japan might even send minesweeping ships to the Gulf as had been suggested in 1987.[11]

In the meantime, Foreign Minister Nakayama, Finance Minister Ryutaro Hashimoto, and Chief of Cabinet Misoji Sakamoto were singled out as particularly engaged in "discussing specific measures to contribute to Middle East peace and stabilization."[12] Professor Seizaburo Sato of the University of Tokyo contributed an article to the *Sankei Shimbun* on the 21 August that later appeared in the 27 August *The Japan Times*. These paragraphs capture some of the views held by the Japanese policy community at the time:

> What is demanded today is action to maintain order to prevent aggression by a dangerous adventurist anywhere in the world. As the second-biggest economic power in the

world, Japan should positively participate in such peace-and-order-maintenance activities, for not doing so will not be in Japan's own interest. Neither will it be acceptable to the rest of the world.

There is still not a little argument in Japan that a nation dedicated to peace should not extend military cooperation but contribute only in the economic area. These people say that as the present Constitution bans the exercise of the right of collective self-defense, sending Self-Defense Force personnel to a place fraught with the danger of a military clash would violate the Constitution, or that neighboring Asian nations would object if Japan cooperated militarily in a distant region.

These arguments reflect unwillingness to do "dangerous, hard and dirty" work. They are selfish and will not be accepted by the world.[13]

Sato went on to call for Japanese participation in rear-support functions such as "communications, supply and medical fields in the Middle East." To do less, in Sato's opinion would open Japan to global criticism.

Foreign Minister Nakayama returned on 25 August from the Middle East. Some of his report was incorporated into the Japanese response of 29 August. Prime Minister Kaifu announced a ten million dollar pledge for Jordan relief, and the next day it was announced that Japan would contribute one billion dollars to the multinational military force being assembled largely under American leadership.

Not all were happy, however. On 4 September the LDP held a leadership conference of chairmen, vice chairmen, and department heads of the Executive Board and the Policy Affairs Research Council, the principal policy formulation centers of the Party. The government response was held "insufficient," leading to more criticism and dissatisfaction among some of the party members.[14]

Approximately one week later, on 7 September, Secretary of the Treasury Nicholas Brady met with Japanese leaders to discuss further assistance that might be offered by Japan for the international effort. Immediately, an additional $12 million was provided for emergency refugee assistance for Jordan, and one week later, Japan announced that two billion dollars would be provided in economic assistance to the states affected by Iraq's action, and that an additional one billion would be pledged for logistic support of the multinational force.

The above did not happen overnight, and involved Congressional shots across the bow, an LDP fact-finding delegation, headed by former Foreign Minister Kuranari, coming to Washington to discuss with US officials our concept of a fair response, and a host of meetings within the LDP-government policy framework.

Not all were pleased, however, and criticism came from the United States and Great Britain. The *Economist* was quoted as wondering if Japan was really "a spineless defective state" in an article in the *Tokyo Shimbun*.[15] The Japanese newspaper was able to note with some pride that the weapons that sustained the Iraqi invasion did not come from Japan. The non-weapon export policy and the denegration of aspects of military power were not seen as necessarily unfortunate.

On 12 October, Prime Minister Kaifu introduced legislation into a special Diet session to permit non-belligerent involvement by " ... people from all walks of life, including Self-Defense Forces and other civil service personnel... "[16] This action demonstrated a political commitment and determination to bring Japan into aspects of international peace-keeping that had not been seen for more than fifty years. In his appeal to the Diet and to the Japanese body politic, Prime Minister Kaifu noted significantly:

> We must never forget that Japan has been one of the prime beneficiaries of the world without war, and it is only when the world is at peace that a resource-poor trading nation such as Japan can enjoy the benefits of prosperity. It must be said that contributing to maintain world peace is both a natural and inevitable cost arising from Japan's position within the international community.[17]

Kaifu's bold backing of this legislation to reinterpret Article 9 of the Constitution was demonstrated leadership. However, it must be remembered that this prime minister comes from the smallest organized faction within the Liberal Democratic Party. His ability to move with the speed we have witnessed is an indication of support within the party, but it also put him in a very exposed position. As mentioned earlier, the ceremonies to mark the accession of the new Emperor were scheduled far in advance of the attempt to introduce the UN peacekeeping legislation into the Diet, and the opposition parties were not at all cooperative. Caught in such a situation, the prime minister admitted defeat and sought to take up the issue in some other form during another session of the Diet.

Critics in the United States who have attacked Japan's response as reflective of "the image of hopeless indecision left by Tokyo's tentative response to Iraqi aggression," only indicate a lack of data or the existence of another agenda that is out of place if we are serious about building a new international order that actually functions as a new international cooperative system.[18]

A Second Call: 17 January 1991

While the world waited and hoped for Iraq to withdraw from Kuwait, the leadership of the Liberal Democratic Party met with the Cabinet on Wednesday night, 16 January, to discuss possible Japanese contributions to the multinational force if war broke out. In a heated exchange some "top leaders of the Liberal Democratic Party 'demanded' ... that Self-Defense Force planes be sent to the Persian Gulf to airlift refugees and Japanese residents from the region ... "[19] Ideas for Japanese assistance also included the dispatching of medical teams to the Gulf.

While reports indicated that Prime Minister Kaifu was "resisting" sending SDF planes to the Gulf, it was also reported that "late Wednesday" (16 January) the Air Self-Defense Force had been instructed to prepare a feasibility study for using C–130s to airlift refugees from Amman and Damascus to Cairo.[20] This also was seen as the first "concrete order" issued to the SDF during the entire Gulf crisis.

The United Nations military reaction to the Iraqi invasion of Kuwait occurred on 17 January 1991, two days after the deadline for a peaceful withdrawal had passed. Prime Minister

Kaifu that day issued a statement following emergency meetings of the Japanese Security Council and Cabinet shortly after air attacks began.[21] In the statement Kaifu said that Japan "strongly" condemned Iraq's blatant invasion and annexation of its neighbor, and pledged Japan's "firm support to the use of force by the countries concerned . . . with UN Security Council Resolution 678 . . . "[22]

In paragraph four of this statement, Kaifu placed Japan directly in support of the UN action:

> Japan is determined to extend maximum possible support, in accordance with the UN Security Council resolutions, to the actions taken by the countries concerned to restore international peace and stability. Furthermore, Japan has decided to offer maximum possible assistance to the evacuees and refugees in cooperation with relevant international organizations and is already taking actions for its implementation.[23]

The speech also included the information that a Gulf Crisis Task Force, headed by the Prime Minister, had been established "within the Cabinet" to manage the response in a "concerted, comprehensive, and effective manner." Kaifu closed the statement by asking for "the understanding and cooperation of all of the people."[24]

According to unnamed "government sources" Japan, at that moment, was considering an additional contribution of four billion dollars to "help defray the allies' military costs."[25]

To enable the Prime Minister to deliver a speech on Japan's policy toward the war, the LDP and the opposition parties agreed to reconvene the Diet on Friday, 18 January 1991, one week ahead of the originally scheduled return from the year-end recess. The Diet members heard an address somewhat longer than the earlier statement with more background details added.

No sooner had the statement of support been released than reporters began to criticize Japan's ability to turn "maximum possible support" into something meaningful. Japan's economic share of the war costs were seen as running from three billion to more than ten. The government was seen as slow to react and uncertain at best about its future course.[26]

"I Was Only Told About This at 8:30 a.m."

Asked by reporters why the government's response seemed less than stellar, Prime Minister Kaifu responded with the words above. Prime Minister Kaifu turned to the task of seeking opposition party support by meeting with the leaders of the five opposition parties on the first evening of the war. Meeting with Takako Doi of the Japan Socialist Party, Koshiro Ishida of Komeito, Tetsuzo Fuwa of the Communist Party, Keigo Ouchi of the Democratic Socialist Party, and Satsuki Eda of the Shaminren he was able to discover that the Komeito and DSP might support additional financial contributions to the multinational force, and that the DSP was the only party that would likely support the air bridge for refugees for the Gulf.[27]

After extensive discussions between the government and leaders of the Liberal Democratic Party, it was announced that on the morning of 25 January, one week after the war began, that Japan had decided to give an additional nine billion dollars to the multinational force, and send Air Self-Defense aircraft to the Gulf to help evacuate individuals in need of assistance. No revision of law was deemed necessary to send the aircraft, only a new ordinance that would limit their involvement to "non-military and humanitarian activities."[28] It was reported that the figure of nine billion was reached in discussions between Nicholas Brady and Finance Minister Ryutaro Hashimoto.

In mid-February 1991 it is clear that the Liberal Democratic Party has worked out a compromise with the Komeito and Democratic Socialist Parties for their support in pushing this legislation through the Diet. We have, in essence, witnessed the second major assistance to the United States since Knokke-Heist and the conference where Japan indicated its desire to be a global partner and assist in the creation of the new international order. If we were to examine Japan's security cooperation in this new international order, we might say first, "Congratulations!"

Second, I think we need to make some organizational or institutional changes that will recognize the new situation. Japan's participation to a greater degree in the United Nations system is being debated and is a very real part of the ongoing defense policy debate in Japan. As we find ourselves using the Iraqi invasion of Kuwait to create a new international security system that perhaps even involves the long-term cooperation of all the Big Five in the UN Military Staff Committee, it is incumbent that we recognize the need for long-term thinking. Irresponsible "Japan bashing" that has become disruptive to the attitudes of both the Japanese and American publics does little to ensure that the Big Five are joined in the new international security system by a responsible Japan.

We need to ensure that the Big Five are, in fact, joined by the defeated states of World War II, both Germany and Japan. Our successful post–World War II policies have led to a restructured Soviet Union, new democracies in Eastern Europe, and economic powers in Japan and Germany. We should now focus on the next fifty years. We must make sure that these countries become permanent members of the Security Council and that the so-called "enemies clause" (which also includes Italy by definition) should be eliminated from the Charter of the United Nations. The Iraqi situation has given us the catalyst to make 1991 an important base for shaping our new security policies; we should not let it pass.

Our experience in the deployment of forces to the Gulf indicates very clearly the importance of having active duty forces forward deployed in certain strategic locations in the world. While the new international system is starting to show its outline as we meet in Hawaii, some portions of the globe have yet to demonstrate that "peace is breaking out all over." One such area is Northeast Asia.

Continuing involvement by the government of Japan in the host nation support program and its willingness to support 100 percent of local costs by the conclusion of the next mid-term defense plan assures that one of the problems toward maintaining a positive working relationship between US forces and the GOJ will be eliminated.

Attempts to restructure the SCC (Security Consultative Committee) to include the US Secretaries of Defense and State assure equal representation on this very important policy consultative body. As can be seen by the late notice to Prime Minister Kaifu in the present crisis, consultation must be seen as a requirement for the future relationship. We should support the democratic practices of the Japanese system and accept the fact that their participation in the new international order will be principally in aid, trade, and economic not military endeavors. That, however, in no way diminishes the importance of involving Japan in the early stages of policy formulation. Perhaps the revised SCC structure will assist in this requirement; it is clear that the United States cannot begin a campaign and deliver the bill to Japan. This will not work. It is the most important area of our new system that requires American attention.

Prime Minister Kaifu, in his speech to the formal opening of the 120th session of the Diet, set out some clear foreign policy goals. He noted:

> Relations with the United States are the cornerstone of Japanese foreign policy. Firm relations of cooperation with the United States are also important in initiating positive foreign policies for peace and prosperity in the Asia-Pacific region and for the construction of a new international order in the world . . . it is imperative that the two countries, as allies, be aware of their shared responsibilities for world peace and prosperity and further strengthen their global partnership of cooperation on global issues.[29]

From the evidence of Japan's participation in the Gulf to date, the new reality of Japanese power leads me to assert that US-Japanese cooperation in the New International Cooperative System has begun and is off to a very productive start. Like all partnerships, it will prosper only if the spirit of continuing reciprocity is honored.

NOTES

1. While the Knokke-Heist Conference was almost unnoticed from an international standpoint, another celebration was also going on to commemorate the 30th anniversary of the signing of the revised US-Japan Security Treaty in 1960. Former Foreign Minister Shintaro Abe was dispatched to Washington to mark the occasion that he remembered with some personal involvement. The 30th anniversary certainly passed more quietly than the signing itself.

2. See John Endicott, "Japanese Security Policy: Stability in an Era of Change?"*Korean Journal of Defense Analysis,* Winter 1991.

3. Such individuals as Motofumi Asai of Tokyo University, Fuji Kamiya of Keio University, Tetsuo Maeda, disarmament specialist, Tadae Takubo of Kyorin University, and others, took part in this phase of the debate, as well as numerous unidentified editorial writers who contributed to the debate before August.

4. *The Japan Times,* 24 April 1990.

5. Hisashi Owada, "Japan's Role in a Multipolar World," Unpublished paper, 8 November 1989, p. 12.

6. *Ibid.*

7. *The Japan Times,* 22 June 1990.

8. Support for the SII Agreement from the business community was a clear indication that the so-called "death of 1000 cuts"—the 301 System to resolve trade disputes—needed to be replaced with a more general examination of the problems of both nations. The SII Agreements in themselves indicated that both governments desired to better prepare the US-Japanese system for the competition from Europe in the 1990s.

9. The NPT Treaty was signed in 1970 and finally ratified on 24 May 1976 after some very active intervention by Prime Minister Miki.

10. *The Japan Times,* 15 August 1990.

11. See *The Japan Times,* for the 15, 18, and 19 August for coverage on these points.

12. *The Japan Times,* 15 August 1990.

13. *The Japan Times,* 27 August 1990.

14. *Sankei Shimbun,* 5 September 1990.

15. *Tokyo Shimbun,* 6 September 1990.

16. *The Japan Times,* 13 October 1990.

17. *Ibid.*

18. *U.S. News and World Report,* 15 October 1990, p. 71.

19. *The Japan Times,* 17 January 1991.

20. *Ibid.* There were newspaper reports that some 550 Japanese remained in the "danger zone" of the Gulf region.

21. *The Japan Times,* 18 January 1991.

22. *Ibid.*

23. *Ibid.*

24. *Ibid.*

25. *Ibid.*

26. *Ibid.*

27. *Ibid.*

28. *Ibid.*

29. *The Japan Times.* 26 January 1991.

FUTURE STRATEGIC OPTIONS IN THE PACIFIC:
PACIFIC:
A NICHIBEI CONDOMINIUM?

Dr. Donald C. Hellmann

Dr. Donald C. Hellmann, *professor at the Henry M. Jackson School of International Studies and the Department of Political Science, University of Washington, holds a B.A. degree from Princeton University and M.A. and Ph.D. degrees from the University of California, Berkeley. He has also taught at Swarthmore College and at Vanderbilt University. He has been a consultant for a number of government agencies and public policy organizations, focussing chiefly on US policy toward Asia, Japan, and the Soviet Union. Dr. Hellmann is a prolific author whose most recent articles are "Old Myths and New Realities: US-Japan Security Relations" and "Japan and the United States in Asia in the Twilight of the Cold War."*

The future security role of the United States in the Pacific can be understood only in the context of the ongoing revolutionary upheaval in the global international landscape. This revolution, temporarily obscured by the events in the Middle East culminating in operation Desert Storm, involves changes of an enormity and an intensity that have parallels in only three other eras of upheaval in the last two hundred years: the aftermaths of the Napoleonic wars of the early 19th century and of World Wars I and II.

The current revolution, dramatically symbolized by an end to the Cold War in the wake of the sudden, cataclysmic collapse of the European communist system, also encompasses a radical shift in economic power, especially to Japan and a reunited Germany. To be sure, the United States remains the only nation capable of effectively projecting political and economic power on a global basis, but clearly it can not do so in the manner of a hegemonic superpower as in the Cold War. There is a need for identifying America's *national* interest with an eye to establishing priorities. Not surprisingly, the sweeping redistribution of economic and political military power over the past five years has severely attenuated or brought about the collapse of many of the international institutions—alliances, multilateral regional and global organizations—devised for managing peace and prosperity during the Cold War era. The Congress of Vienna, the Versailles peace agreements (including the League of Nations), and both the United Nations and *Pax Americana,* all created fresh institutional arrangements appropriate to the new distribution of international power.

The visions of world order embodied in each of these efforts at institution-building eventually broke down. The breakdowns were mandated by changed economic and political conditions and the changes in the nature of international mores prevalent in the international system (from imperialism to nationalism, from coalitions among equal states to hegemonic military alliances). Because we are today in the throes of transition to a new international era, in considering future strategic options it is essential to go back to basics and not merely tinker with increasingly anachronistic alliances and force projections. It is a time for vision and leadership in the manner displayed in earlier eras of upheaval.

In the aftermath of World War II, these hortatory remarks would have been superfluous because those people of influence in Washington who asked and answered questions about the future strategic role of the United States in the Pacific and the world were rightly seen as "architects of America's century."[1] A similar bold, historically rooted but visionary and architectonic approach is essential today. Alas, the current tide of official reports (for example, The White House, *The National Security Strategy of the United States,* March 1990), structured ruminations about policy in international affairs journals, or the independent studies and commissioned reports from "think tanks", display little of the imagination and verve seen in the years immediately after World War II. Despite the global prevalence of American power in the immediate future, we stand at risk of leadership in the "new world order" because of a collective problem with the vision thing. This is readily illustrated with regard to our strategic role in the Pacific.

A Nichi-bei Condominium?

Gordus, the father of Midas, became the dominant political power in Phrygia (Asia). His authority and the political and economic welfare of the region was secured and symbolized by an intricate knot. It was said that whoever untied this Gordian knot would become the lord of Asia.
Midas, the offspring of Gordus, was granted by the gods one wish for anything he wanted. Midas wished that whatever he touched would turn to gold. Dismayed that this power prevented him from leading his realm, or even eating, he quickly implored that the favor be taken back.

Editor's note. The Japanese characters that the term "Nichibei" represents can be written either with or without the hyphen. Without the hyphen a greater degree of closeness is implied.

Midas, whose name has become a synonym for a rich man, is also a symbol of folly especially for those who would be leaders.

Adapted from Edith Hamilton, *Mythology,*
Timeless Tales of Gods and Heroes

The complex web of military alliances, international institutions, ad hoc economic transactions and political security actions that have defined the American presence in East Asia since World War II may be seen as a modern-day Gordian knot. Throughout turbulent decades of war, revolution and upheaval, the American knot provided a framework of security, stability, and economic opportunity that facilitated the astonishing transformation of what was a war-ravaged, largely post-colonial international backwater into the most rapidly expanding economic region in the world. The benefits are unevenly distributed among the nations of East Asia, but there is no doubt that the country that benefited most from *Pax Americana* in the Pacific is Japan.

If the United States can be seen as a contemporary Gordus, Japan is the modern-day Midas. During the seven-year occupation of Japan, the United States undertook comprehensive reforms to restructure and democratize all aspects of Japanese society, writing a new constitution and instituting radical and sweeping economic and social reforms. In the ensuing decades, Japan, Midas-like, matured as a kind of democratic-capitalist offspring of the United States—a close anti-communist ally, a defense satellite in the Cold War, and a salubriously interdependent economic partner. Sheltered within an American-made security greenhouse and nourished by the American-dominated free trade oriented international economic order, Japan developed a golden touch. From an impoverished international economic basketcase (the consensus judgment of all observers in the early 1950s), Japan in 1990 had become by far the largest creditor nation in the world, with a per capita GNP thirty per cent greater than that in the United States and an aggregate GNP almost one and one half times that of the Soviet Union. The Cold War era made Japan an economic superpower. Qualitatively, the achievements and the promise are equally astonishing in terms of global leadership in technology as well as finance. If the basic structure of the world economy in the next decade remains essentially as it has in the recent past, there is consensus judgment that Japan will continue to outperform the other major industrial powers by a significant margin. Moreover, in an accelerating fashion the Japanese have come to dominate trade, investment, and aid in the most rapidly developing region in the world—East Asia.

Nevertheless, extrapolations of an impending Japanese economic order by both the critics and the defenders of Japan rarely take into account that Tokyo's golden touch has been dependent on an international political-security order created by *Pax Americana* . It was the willingness of the United States to maintain stability in the world that permitted Japan to develop in a unidimensional economic fashion during the decades since World War II, an era of global strategic confrontation and regional war and revolution. However brilliant the economic leadership by MITI and the technocrats, it was possible only because of the international greenhouse made in America. Obviously, the preferred position for Tokyo is a continuation of this free ride on the back of the United States with regard to all matters of international conflict, be it "containment"or global police actions. There are numerous (and subsequently elaborated) political and economic constraints making this highly unlikely and unless you make the radical assumption that international political conflicts will effectively retreat to the periphery of world affairs, some nation or combination of nations will have to emerge to maintain order in the post-Cold War world. By any historically rooted criteria, Japan, currently the world's most dynamic and successful economic power, must bear a huge part of the burden to maintain world order to facilitate prosperity. And here's the rub. Further corroborating the details of the myth, Japan's affluence is accompanied by a Midas-like incapacity for international leadership that is rooted in a reluctance and/or an inability to define in a credible way a national purpose beyond narrow economic self-interest.

In the latter part of the 1980s, the present-day Gordian knot, *Pax Americana* in the Pacific (and the world), began to unravel. First, the sudden collapse of East European and Soviet communism led to a fundamental redefinition of global security. Second, a dramatic shift in international economic power involving, *inter alia,* the substantial relative decline of the United States and the rise of Japan, severely inhibited the capacity of America to continue as a global political-economic hegemon in the pattern of the recent past. Because this unraveling was brought about not by a calculated policy choice by the new "lord of Asia," but by basic changes in the structure of the global political economy, the international situation is fluid and indeterminate. With the end of the prolonged postwar era finally at hand, Japan and the United States must now confront the emerging realities of a transformed world. Both the political-security and the economic relationship between Gordus and Midas must be reconstructed.

In the post-Cold War world a viable adjustment of Japanese-American relations requires the effective linkage of economic and strategic policy considerations. The hegemonic security alliance now operative was crafted in the early years of the Cold War when Japan was a devastated and poor society under American military occupation. The alliance is an anachronism. It is structured on assumptions about Japanese power and international behavior appropriate to the years immediately after World War II and on the international role of the United States during the height of the Cold War in the 1950s and early 1960s.

Perpetuation of the anachronistic asymmetry of this relationship has in recent years led to numerous astonishing and inherently nonviable results: the world's largest debtor nation effectively underwrites the security of the world's largest creditor; Japan does not participate in the United Nations or any multilateral overseas military activities despite the world's third largest defense force that is legitimated by appeal to the United Nations' charter. These international anomalies, together with persistent and protracted bilateral friction over trade and investment, have provoked a strongly negative and increasingly populist political reaction in the United States. Hostile Congressional actions have grown in number and intensity as occurred in the FSX incident. Public opinion polls replace the Soviet Union with Japan as the greatest threat to the United States. The American media have taken an increasingly adversarial position regarding Japan. These developments have introduced a volatile new variable into bilateral relations and make the policy challenge for the US President twofold: to bring the American-Japanese relationship into greater congruence with the new international realities of the post-Cold War world and at the same time to reestablish leadership on this issue in American domestic politics.

Any Japanese government that undertakes a fundamental restructuring of relations with the United States must respond to the changes in international conditions attendant on the end of the Cold War. It will also face a major challenge in domestic policy leadership. In the United States, this task involves a fundamental overhaul of strategic and policy priorities; for Japan, the challenge is even more daunting. On the one hand, it involves no less than defining a new national purpose that is more than the unidimensional, Midas-like aim of maximizing national economic self-interest. On the other hand, the implementation of policies appropriate to a new national purpose will require a kind of Japanese *perestroika* of the institutions of foreign policymaking that have been dominated by a bureaucratic-business-party elite for almost half a century. The comprehensive and revolutionary nature of this challenge, plus the fact that there is little incentive to change a successful formula, makes it highly improbable that Japan will emerge in the immediate future as an independent international leader either in East Asia or the world, without a breakdown or radical restructuring of the Japanese-US alliance.

The Military Component of the Nichi-Bei Condominium Does it make sense to even discuss a regional military role for Japan? Domestically, the Japanese claim it is unconstitutional for them to participate even in UN sanctioned peacekeeping. Opinion polls indicate that over eighty percent of the Japanese public oppose an *overseas* military role for the country and the current party configuration in the Diet would block any policy move in this direction. Internationally, there is near unanimity among Asian states opposing an overseas military role for Japan—even in the Persian Gulf. Astonishingly, Pentagon reports, public statements by American military leaders, and virtually all assessments of the future military role of Japan in the Pacific agree that the US security commitment to Japan links Tokyo to American goals and interests in the region while also reassuring states throughout the Pacific that they will not have to confront Japanese economic as well as military might.[2]

Japan is thus seen as a militarist nation, incapable of behaving in a responsible and orthodox way by militarily contributing to world peace and the US-Japan alliance is viewed as the cap on the bottle restraining the genie of Japanese nationalism. To assume continuation of the enormous discontinuities between Japanese economic and political power, because of an implied flaw in Japan's national character manifested in behavior during World War II has an Alice in Wonderland quality that is singularly inappropriate if Japan is to be included, with appropriate responsibilities, in a new world order.

A new world and Pacific order is inevitable and there are compelling reasons for the United States to move expeditiously to integrate Japan into fresh institutions for maintaining international order. Although the United Nations proved to be a convenient venue for conducting Operation Desert Storm, the entire UN peacekeeping mechanism (especially membership in the Security Council) would have to be drastically overhauled to be viable in the long run. Historically, the UN is merely the most recent effort of the winning coalition of nations in a major war to devise a general scheme for maintaining peace. Two of the losers in World War II, Japan and Germany, are now the dominant economic powers in Europe and Asia and it is folly to imagine any future world order without the full (military as well as economic) participation of the Japanese and Germans. In view of the end of the Cold War and persistent, widespread social and economic problems in the United States, there will be substantial, perhaps massive, reductions in American defense expenditures in the immediate future. Without a new strategic mission to guide such cuts, the future strategic direction will be established by budgetary trade-offs, political deals in the corridors of power in Washington, or on agenda set by ad hoc responses to international crises (such as the current crisis in the Gulf). Burden-sharing is power sharing and any viable long-term relation realistically accounting for

American and Japanese nationalism must move beyond hegemonic or "neo-mercenary" patterns of cooperation.

Any new strategic order in East Asia must include the dominant regional power, Japan, but it is only under the leadership of the United States that change in the status quo will come about. This was graphically illustrated in the Gilbert and Sullivan character of the response of Tokyo to American pressure to join the coalition. Prime Minister Kaifu refused to provide even symbolic military participation in an action President Bush called the prototype of a new world order, citing three reasons. First, the Constitution, which clearly permits dispatch of military forces to UN sponsored peacekeeping activities (Article 9 was rewritten by the Japanese in 1947 for that purpose), was used as an excuse to avoid power politics. Secondly, Kaifu said public opinion was shown in opinion polls to be strongly pacificist and that this placed ineluctable limits on government policy—despite the fact that for four decades the government brilliantly designed and managed a foreign economic policy that involved protracted and excessive manipulation of the consumer. Thirdly, the intra- and interparty stalemate in the Diet was said to obviate any action involving the dispatch of troops. This literally was true, but reflected more on the personal leadership abilities of Kaifu and the severe limitations on the Japanese political system to display flexibility in the face of crisis. Throughout the postwar era, Japan has displayed similar immobilism when faced with major political issues in foreign policy (such as normalization of relations with the Soviet Union and China, and renewal of the United States security treaty in 1960.) Accordingly, if the United States is to bring Japan into a new strategic order, sustained and sophisticated pressure *(gaiatsu)* on Tokyo is the most effective way to proceed. The emphasis, even more so after the victory over Saddam Hussein, should be on an "alliance dividend" owed to the United States for more than forty years of military involvement in the region.

There is one obvious way to redefine American policy in keeping with tangible Asian security needs, the enhanced economic power of nations in the region, and the obvious need for a new security system to supplant the anachronistic alliances and base structure now in place. Security in the Pacific is moving from hegemony to what may be called complex strategic interdependence. There are three dimensions to the new strategic realities. On one level, the strategic nuclear balance remains the preserve of the military superpowers and will be addressed in the current ongoing arms control negotiations as well as in traditional power balancing maneuvers. The second level, involving territorial defense, will serve as a touchstone for the boundaries of nationalism in each country and will move, throughout Asia, from hegomony toward partnership.

"Constabulary security" is the third strategic dimension. It refers to the needs for a regional and/or global police force. There are compelling reasons for such a force:

- the need to respond to ad hoc crises in order to facilitate economic intercourse;

- the demand for force in addressing issues such as terrorism, the drug war, or "renegade" regimes (such as Noriega, Saddam Hussein); and

- the need to protect the sealanes to the Middle East.

To finance and staff such activities would necessitate an international institutional *perestroika*—a multilateral alliance framework constructed to share political as well as economic risks and costs. In Asia, such an arrangement would facilitate ending the "free ride" Japan has been having in the international system and could serve as the bridge to bring the Soviet Union and other communist states into a redefined security set-up with reciprocal and mutual benefits. It is absurd for the United States to guarantee the security of sealanes in which more than ninety-five percent of the ships are not American. Were these responsibilities internationalized along with the bases—such as Subic Bay—involved, a constructive and compelling redefinition of security would be put into place.

This initiative would move toward bringing Japan into a more responsible and acceptable military role without igniting the flames of Japanese nationalism. It is a policy initiative open only to the United States for, despite an enormous expansion of economic power throughout the region, Japan remains virtually a pariah state in matters of security and politics. The shadow Japan casts over much of East Asia in the decades ahead is in many ways the most uncertain and threatening component of the new international era. If the United States fails to provide a new strategic framework for solving this problem, many of the achievements of the past four decades will be squandered. A multi-lateral effort in constabulary security, however broad its membership, could well evolve into American-Japanese partnership. The Nichibei Condominium is an appropriate replacement for *Pax Americana* in the Pacific.

NOTES

1. See, for example, Walter Isaacson and Evan Thomas, *The Wise Men,* Simon and Shuster, 1986.

2. Jonathan D. Pollack and James A. Winnefeld, *US Strategic Alternatives in a Changing Pacific (*RAND Corporation, June 1990), p. 14.

THE KOREAN PENINSULA IN A CHANGING ENVIRONMENT: PROSPECTS FOR PEACE AND UNIFICATION

Dr. Lee Young Ho

Dr. Lee Young Ho holds B.A. degrees from Yonsei University and Amherst College and a Ph.D. from Yale University. He taught at the University of Georgia, Athens, before returning to Korea to hold positions in policy research and to become Assistant Minister for Policy Planning, National Unification Board, and Professor of Political Science, Ewha Women's University Seoul. After being Minister of Sports Dr. Lee held the position of Executive President, Seoul Olympic Organizing Committee. He is currently chairman and president of the Korea Policy Research Institute in Seoul.

I am particularly happy that the Gulf War will probably have some important, beneficial effect on the Korean peninsula. The way the United Nations and particularly the United States and allies have reacted to Saddam Hussein's invasion of Kuwait, and the way the coalition forces have brought the Gulf War to a successful conclusion will have a very sobering effect on Kim Il Sung and other North Korean leaders who at present constitute practically the sole major source of military instability in the Korean peninsula. The Gulf War has convincingly demonstrated the superiority of US weapons which constitute a central element in the South Korean arsenal and also, very importantly, demonstrated the credibility of US security commitments.

Another consequence of the war may be that President George Bush will be a shoo-in in next year's US presidential elections and occupy the White House until 1997. By then, Kim Il Sung will be nearly 85 years of age, if he lives that long. The Bush presidency will probably make the North Korean leadership, whether in the hands of Kim Il Sung or someone else, think twice or thrice before mounting another military venture against South Korea. The Republic of Korea has never harbored an aggressive intention toward North Korea, because it has so much to lose in another Korean War, in terms of lives and property, even if it were to achieve a final military victory. For the South, the price to be paid is too high for whatever were attained through such a conflict.

In contrast, we cannot be certain of North Korea's commitment to non-aggression. Ever since its establishment in 1948, the North Korean regime has been pursuing a military-revolutionary strategy toward South Korea. To achieve unification on its own terms, the regime's strategy envisions engaging in offensive military operations against the South while simultaneously instigating a revolutionary upheaval within South Korea to support the military operations. The only reason it has not put such a strategy into action again since its first unsuccessful attempt in the Korean War (1950–1953) is because the situation has not been ripe for such an action.

(There is ample evidence to support this conclusion, but I do not intend to go into a detailed discussion of North Korea's aggressive intentions here.)

Recently, some signs of an increasing timidity or cautiousness have been evident on the part of North Korea. We hope that this timidity will soon turn into a more definite commitment to a policy of peaceful resolution of the Korean question. What are the possible causes for North Korea's increasing cautiousness?

First, South Korea is fast achieving a military parity with North Korea on the strength of its vigorously growing economy. South Korea's GNP is at least ten times as large as North Korea's, and the gap continues to widen. Therefore, although it devotes a much smaller proportion of its GNP to defense, South Korea still has a much bigger defense budget—in absolute terms.

Second, the United States is not withdrawing its troops from South Korea fast enough, or reducing its military presence in South Korea fast enough to give North Korea the opportunity to take a decisive military offensive while South Korea remains weaker militarily in comparison with North Korea. Furthermore, the Gulf War will most likely make US security commitments to the Republic of Korea much more credible.

Third, like Saddam Hussein's Iraq in the Gulf War, North Korea no longer has sources of ready outside support for weapons and other war-related materials to rely upon in the event it undertakes a major military venture. Neither the Soviet Union nor China is likely to provide ready support for North Korea should it initiate another war on the peninsula. Both these traditional North Korean allies have substantially readjusted their policy toward the Korean peninsula. The Soviet Union has opened diplomatic relations and seeks expanding economic cooperation with the Republic of Korea. China has exchanged trade missions and seeks to further expand its already substantial economic cooperation with South Korea. Neither country would want to risk jeopardizing its improving relations with the United States and Japan by supporting North Korea's military aggression. There are indications that both countries are trying to persuade North Korea to adopt a more conciliatory posture toward South Korea.

Finally, South Korea's political stability must also serve as another factor for North Korea's cautiousness. The revolutionary dimension of North Korea's military-revolutionary strategy is predicated upon political instability within South Korea. There has been a long record of instability in the south which must have raised the hopes of the North Korean leadership. However, South Korea took major steps in democratization in the late eighties. As a result, though South Korea's politics today are noisier than ever, and its government subjected to all kinds of criticism—sometimes even to downright ridicule— and although its opposition is increasingly outspoken, the political system as a whole enjoys popular support and stability. There is today no revolutionary undercurrent in South Korean society strong enough for North Korea to take advantage of in pursuit of its military-revolutionary strategy. There are, certainly, some pro-North Korean elements in South Korea but in all probability they do not constitute a significant base of support for North Korea.

There are other factors that will, in the long run, contribute to the causes of peace and unification on the Korean peninsula. North Korea's economy is in very serious trouble. As I mentioned earlier, North Korea's economy is no match for South Korea's, and the gap is widening. We hear of serious shortages in necessities such as food and clothing in North Korea. The country has been in arrears in honoring its external debts. North Korea's major traditional benefactors, the Soviet Union and China, finding themselves enmeshed in their own economic difficulties, are not in a position to help. North Korea badly needs foreign investments. But significant foreign investments will not be forthcoming as long as it refuses to introduce economic reforms internally, to improve relations with South Korea, and reduce tension on the Korean peninsula.

For economic as well as political reasons, North Korea would very much like to normalize relations with Japan and the United States. North Korea's normalization with Japan would somewhat offset South Korea's establishment of diplomatic relations with the Soviet Union and other East European nations. It would also mean a large reparations sum for Japan's 35-year colonial rule. South Korea received $500 million in reparation payment when it normalized relations with Japan in 1964. That amount may translate into some $2 billion in current prices. Normalization with Tokyo would also open the way for Japanese private investments in North Korea.

Normalization talks are currently under way. However, Tokyo seems to take the position that it should not go ahead with normalization until North Korea agrees to International Atomic Energy Agency (IAEA) safeguards requirements and significantly improves relations with South Korea. Tokyo also seems eager to make sure that whatever economic assistance it gives North Korea does not find a way into military use. It looks as though the normalization talks will go on much longer than Pyongyang hopes before concrete agreements are signed.

Pyongyang also wishes to expand and, in the end, normalize relations with the United States. This would balance out Seoul's establishment of diplomatic relations with East European capitals, most notably Moscow. It would also improve the atmosphere for US and other firms to invest in North Korea. However, Washington seems even less eager than Tokyo to improve relations with Pyongyang before any significant breakthroughs are made in North-South Korean relations.

Domestic pressure for economic reforms is mounting in North Korea. Deteriorating living conditions are a major source of such pressure. What aggravates the situation even further is that North Koreans are increasingly exposed to outside information and are becoming aware of the changes taking place outside North Korea. They learn of the sweeping reforms the East European nations have undertaken in recent years and wonder whether North Korea, too, should not take such a path. They also learn that living conditions in South Korea are quite the opposite of what the North Korean official propaganda machine has pictured. One important source of information about the outside world (particularly South Korea) for North Koreans is their rather frequent contacts with Korean residents living in China and the Soviet Union, just across from the borders. Such information, coupled with the harsh conditions of existence in their own country, has given rise to their increasing disaffection with their leadership and their desire for change.

This discontent on the part of the North Korean populace still remains largely subterranean. But noticed and perceived by the leadership, it becomes a powerful source of pressure for the regime to do better for the people. There are also signs that popular discontent does come to the surface now and then. Yet the North Korean regime cannot afford to go into its own *glasnost* and *perestroika* full swing because such reforms involve opening the society to the outside world and such an opening could very likely lead to a too explosive or uncontrollable situation. The regime is not ready to take such a risk.

Hence, North Korea's double stance, being firm against reforms internally and at least seemingly flexible externally. Even though Pyongyang recently has made various overtures to South Korea, they seem dubiously motivated at best. In relation to South Korea, Pyongyang proposed, or expressed a willingness to accept, a non-aggressive agreement, arms reduction and control measures, an agreement to form single North-South Korean entries in international sports competitions in table tennis and junior soccer, and various North-South Korean talks, including prime ministerial meetings. But it is unrealistic to view all these as evidence that North Korea is finally committed to peaceful coexistence and cooperation with South Korea.

North Korea talks peace but its deeds bespeak a continued adherence to a strategy of military-revolutionary resolution of the problem of national division. It keeps its main military units forward-deployed, allowing almost no early warning to South Korea. There has been no letdown in its hostile propaganda and other subversive activities against South Korea. Even its vocal denunciation of the annual ROK-US Team Spirit military exercise must be viewed as double-faced. If it really sees a serious aggressive intent in the exercise, it should accept the long-standing invitation to send an observation team to verify whether Team Spirit is offensive or defensive in nature.

Despite North Korea's stubborn desire to stick to the military-revolutionary strategy of unification, trends within and without the Korean peninsula are becoming increasingly unfavorable. Granted there is the possibility of a setback in the Soviet Union's political and economic reforms. But democracy and market economy will likely constitute the mega-trends of the world in the nineties, and the Soviet Union will not be an exception, whatever Mikhail Gorbachev's political fortune may be. China, too, will likely move toward, rather than away from democracy and a market-oriented economy in the coming years. This means that the world is entering a post-Cold War era. This foreshadows mounting pressure on North Korea to change both its internal political and economic policy and its policy toward South Korea.

Within the Korean peninsula, despite some immediate political and economic problems, South Korea is likely to become politically more democratic and stable, and stronger economically. As a result, the military gap between North and South will soon be closed and the situation reversed if some effective arms control regime is not put in place. Thus, an opportunity for North Korea to implement its military-revolutionary strategy will not likely open up. In short, time is not on North Korea's side. It is on South Korea's side—on the side of peace and eventual peaceful unification.

I am of the view that a durable peace on the Korean peninsula is not so distant. It may even be just around the corner. If we successfully manage the immediate future in the next few years, we will be able to build a relatively firm basis for durable peace. In a few years from now, South Korea will most probably have a much stronger capability to deter, assuming that the United States continues to maintain security commitments even if at a reduced level. South Korea's growing democratic stability and economic superiority should convince the North Korean leadership that the military competition is a losing proposition. Still, we are not there yet. We are not in the late nineties or in the 21st century. In 1991, we still have the task of managing these few years without allowing North Korea to be too tempted to take the military-revolutionary option.

In meeting this challenge, the four major countries in the region, namely the United States, the Soviet Union, China, and Japan, as well as the Republic of Korea, each has an important role to play. The Republic of Korea must continue to improve its defense capability while engaging North Korea in various efforts to turn North-South confrontation and competition into coexistence and cooperation. It must make a particular effort to put in place tension-reducing and confidence-building measures. At the same time, it must continue to create an even better society for its people to live in. For a stable, affluent, and contented society is the best basis for national security.

The United States must continue to maintain a credible level of security commitment to the Republic of Korea. A peaceful and stable Korean peninsula is in the national interest of the United States as well. Without a stable peninsula Asia-Pacific peace is impossible. Besides, the United States has so much at stake, economically as well as politically, in the Republic of Korea's security and equilibrium.

In future contacts with Pyongyang, Washington's top priority should be to persuade the North Korean regime to turn their swords into plowshares, and to adopt a policy of peaceful coexistence and cooperation rather than military confrontation and revolutionary subversion. South Korea should not object to the United States or Japan giving economic help to North Korea provided that such help is not diverted to military uses.

Among the issues in Japan's normalization negotiations with North Korea are the question of Japan's apologies for the past wrongdoing (colonial rule); the amount and form of reparation for colonial exploitation; and the question of North Korea's failure to agree to IAEA safeguards requirements. Japan should be as forthright and repentant as possible in its apologies, and as magnanimous as possible in reparation. At the same time, Japan should be absolutely steadfast in demanding North Korea's agreement to International Atomic Energy Agency requirements as a precondition for normalization. Japan should also insist on some safety mechanism to ensure that the money and material it provides to North Korea as part of the normalization/reparation package are not used for military purposes. Japan also should see to it that normalization talks with Pyongyang keep pace with the progress of inter-Korean relations. In other words, normalization should be exploited as leverage to induce North Korea to improve relations with South Korea as well as adopt internal political and economic reforms as much as possible.

The Soviet Union and China also have an important stake in peace on the Korean peninsula. Lately, South Korea has become a significant economic partner for both these traditional allies of North Korea. Any increase in instability on the peninsula is likely to strain such partnerships. As I mentioned earlier, there are indications that both these countries have lately been exerting some moderating influence on Pyongyang. They should keep it up.

If South Korea and the four major countries in the region each play their respective role properly, peace on the peninsula should not be such an elusive goal. Korea may even be able to enter the new century, only nine years from now, not divided as it is now but as a reunified nation enjoying peace, prosperity, and freedom.

I mention here freedom as well as peace and prosperity because I envision a democratic unification. We can think of various scenarios for Korean unification, such as, military takeover by the North; military takeover by the South; negotiated settlement; peaceful absorption by the North; and peaceful absorption by the South. Without going into a detailed discussion of these alternative ways of unification suffice it to say that the last mentioned method of unification, absorption by the South, appears most feasible.

As in the case of the former East Germany, the North Korean regime has a good chance of going down in the near future. It is a regime built on falsehood. When the light of truth penetrates the society, as will be inevitable, the regime may crumble as quickly as darkness evaporates in the face of morning sunlight. The people in North Korea will likely start demanding a better lot, politically and economically, than they enjoy under the existing regime. In the interim of fast transition, people power may prevail, with the people dictating to the leadership, rather than vice versa. The people will likely see a better future in joining South Korea through a democratic process.

Without ruling out other possibilities, I am only expressing the view that unification through absorption by the South seems to have the greatest possibility. I am not ruling out efforts for a negotiated settlement; such efforts should be continued and even redoubled. Whether negotiations alone will bring about unification or not, they will only strengthen the possibility of unification by absorption if it has to come to that in the end.

Today, we are celebrating the great victory by the coalition forces in the Gulf War. I hope the day will come soon when we celebrate the attainment of durable peace—and peaceful unification—on the Korean peninsula. We all have a task to help usher in such a future. We can take heart from the fact that considerable progress has already been made toward peace and unification.

AUSTRALIA'S POLITICAL AND STRATEGIC INTERESTS IN THE PACIFIC IN THE 1990s

Dr. Harry G. Gelber

Dr. Harry G. Gelber was educated at Eltham College and Cambridge and Monash Universities. He was a foreign correspondent for Reuters and the **Times** (London) before becoming an academic. He has been a visiting fellow or professor at Harvard, Yale, George Washington, Oxford, and Cambridge Universities, and at the London School of Economics. He has written widely on strategic and foreign policy matters and on higher education issues. His books include **The Australian-American Alliance; Technology, Defence, and External Relations in China, 1975-78;** and **Universities: Problems and Prospects** for the Institute of Public Affairs, Melbourne. Dr. Gelber has served on a number of government commissions and as a consultant to various agencies. He is presently Professor of Political Science at the University of Tasmania in Hobart.

We have lived through a time of singular turmoil on the international stage. The dramatic changes were not confined to the realms of politics and strategy. By the end of the 1980s it was becoming clear that none of the old national or even international mechanisms for the management of money and credit retained their efficacy. Even the question what money is, seemed frequently unanswerable. No state could any longer manage or guarantee the value of its own currency. Even joint management of money matters, as in the Louvre or Plaza accords of the earlier 1980s, turned out to run into, even to cause, great difficulties. Questions of trade and foreign investment were equally becoming less manageable or even understood. Questions like "what is a firm?" or "who owns this entity?" or "what technologies have gone into the production of this and where do these technologies or components come from?" often seemed equally unanswerable. More facets of international and even national economic activity were not just uncontrolled but in some sense uncontrollable, certainly by public authorities.

It is hardly surprising that in Australia governmental and political opinion formation and, *a fortiori,* policy development, should have lagged behind these rapidly moving events. With respect to many issues, and most parts of the world, Australian policy is of necessity reactive. Even generalities, and certainly most details of policy, depend upon a more or less reliable identification of the positions of others and of political trends. The events of 1989–91 were bound to produce major reappraisals of, if not confusion about, many of the assumptions which have underpinned policy.

There are, at the time of writing, critically important questions about the future of US policy as and when matters settle down after the Gulf War. One scenario might be that if the Gulf War is settled relatively quickly and—from the coalition's point of view—without undue cost in lives and morale, the outcome might include an increased role for the UN Security Council, with US backing as a kind of managing director and even enforcer, as a moral and political power combination which few other states would be in a position to confront. But it is also possible that US public and congressional disappointment with the seemingly half-hearted performance of some allies, together with the large financial burdens of the war, will strengthen the tendencies to withdraw from the world which are never far below the surface of US politics. Much will also depend upon the future of the Soviet Union. A fragmentation of the Soviet empire, together perhaps with effective German influence in large parts of Eastern Europe, might strengthen the American wish to draw down forces and responsibilities in Western Europe. On the other hand, severe internal conflicts or else a reassertion of central and Party power in Moscow, together with repression of dissidence in some of the republics, might have the opposite effect. Similarly, continuing doubts about Soviet good faith in fulfilling arms control agreements could lead to fears of revived dangers posed by the Soviet Union to Europe, the Pacific, and even the United States. These and other possibilities could powerfully affect the character of future US relations not only with Moscow and the European Community (EC), but with the two Koreas and perhaps even with Japan. The strategic future of the Pacific clearly depends critically on the answers to these and other such questions. The future of relations between Japan and the United States is, of course, of special importance to Australia, which has vital political and trading interests at stake in and with both countries.

In that general context, the Gulf crisis offers some particularly interesting and direct insights into Australia's approach to, and conduct of, external and national security affairs. Following the Iraqi invasion of Kuwait, Australia came almost immediately to the support of the United States and of the anti-Iraqi coalition. The Prime Minister spoke of the grave nature of the crisis and its great importance to Australia. In joining the blockade of Iraq, Australia sacrificed important trading interests with that country and perhaps other areas of the Middle East. Two frigates and one supply ship were dispatched to the area and later joined a US carrier group in the Gulf. It was the first time in Australia's history that any Labor Government had sent forces abroad on such a mission. The House of Representatives voted, with only one dissenting voice, to support the commitment and this bipartisan support was maintained following the start of the fighting in January 1991. Public opinion polls, and the media, showed large-scale support for the Gulf coalition. However, some sections of opinion and, more importantly, of the parliamentary Labor Party and the federal bureaucracy, remained unconvinced that the affair impinged directly on Australia's chief concerns or that young Australians should be put in harm's way over the issue. Nevertheless, the general course of events demonstrates that, when confronted by major international disturbances, Australian governments (and opposition parties) are willing to revert to the classic Australian view that the nation's fate is bound up with major shifts in the balance of global power; and that Australia has interests as well as obligations at stake in supporting her major allies.

However, the crisis also highlighted certain weaknesses in Australian political attitudes and military planning. Australia's military contribution in the Gulf has been very small, certainly in relation to the government's claims as to the seriousness of the issues. The trouble, largely unacknowledged in public debate, is not just that there is some dispute in governmental circles about how far Australia should get involved, but that there is not very much more that Australia could do even if the government wanted to. Australia does not have much military force to send, and could not afford serious damage to her force overseas. The Army could field a light, mobile force but nothing even of brigade size could be dispatched and no heavy or armored forces are available. The Air Force could send some F–18s and Australia has some two dozen F–111s but they represent, at present, Australia's sole striking force for the defense of Australia. The two frigates sent to the Gulf are part of an operational establishment of about nine. Altogether, any more serious contribution in the Gulf campaign would run into insoluble problems of reinforcement in the event of battle damage or casualties.

The entire affair, therefore, sharply illustrates some fundamental dilemmas of contemporary Australian external and strategic policy. The configuration of an armed force whose principal task is the defense of Australia is distinctly different from that of a force whose task is likely to be an overseas expedition. To try to do both would greatly exceed the resource allocations which any recent Australian government has been willing to make to defense. And yet, in spite of 15 years of governmental emphasis on the self-reliant defense of Australia, on the first occasion since the Vietnam war that any Australian government has wanted to use military forces (and with the exception of minor UN peacekeeping contributions) it has been for an overseas purpose very different from that for which the Australian Defence Force was said to be chiefly, if not exclusively, designed.

An associated difficulty is political. In relation to the gravity of the issues which the government of the day said were at stake, the Australian contributions in Korea, in Vietnam, and elsewhere, as well as in the Gulf, have been remarkably small. There is some danger that Australian parliaments and bureaucracies will become accustomed to expecting great political resonance at home, as well as great diplomatic benefits abroad from contributions in human and material resource allocation which are really very minor. Great external expectations on the basis of rather narrow and limited Australian will and capabilities seems an unlikely prescription for a successful national foreign policy in the longer term.

Difficulties of this kind might be reflected even in areas relatively close to Australia. Governments have repeatedly acknowledged commitments to Papua New Guinea, for example, or to some areas of the South Pacific. But what is it that Australia could actually do in the event of some larger kinds of security crisis? Suppose, for instance, that there were serious internal or external difficulties in Papua New Guinea, would its government really be reassured by Canberra's capacity to send, at most, a couple of battalions of infantry and a few aircraft or helicopters?

Events in the Indian Ocean and Southeast Asia, present Australian external affairs and security planners with other questions. While the Indian Ocean has traditionally been a matter of much less concern than the South Pacific or Southeast Asia, a number of more recent developments are changing that situation. The political and strategic importance of the Straits of Ormuz needs no emphasis. Nor does the relationship between India and Pakistan. But the general and especially naval expansion of India's forces is a relatively new phenomenon of interest to Malaysia, Indonesia, and Singapore, as well as to Australia herself. And while it would be inappropriate to consider that naval expansion as necessarily creating problems for Australia or her immediate neighborhood, it certainly changes existing patterns in a way which Australians will continue to watch. The more so as India has given signals in the past that it might be willing to play a protective role in relation to ethnic Indian groups in areas like Africa or Fiji.

Australian relations with Indonesia are sufficiently amicable and seem likely to remain so, since both sides regard that situation as highly desirable. All major political groups in Australia regard good relations with Indonesia as being of prime importance, although some sections of the intellectual community and the media worry from time to time about certain aspects of Indonesian affairs and policies—for instance, in East Timor. For the time being, the areas of more serious concern in Southeast Asia will remain Vietnam and Cambodia. Australia has, for some time, taken the view that the Western world should, in its own interests, offer to Hanoi some alternative to its long dependence on, or links with, the Soviet Union. The principle remains, reinforced rather than weakened by more recent changes in Soviet policy and cohesion, the decline of Soviet power and Vietnam's patent need for economic reform and external aid. The question of timing, on the other hand, is clearly not one which Australia can control, but is rather in the hands of the United States, ASEAN and, of course, China. As for Cambodia, Australia seems likely to continue to try to play a special role. The government has given every sign of willingness not merely to engage itself heavily in the issue of a Cambodian settlement, but to send Australian troops there as part of a peacekeeping force once appropriate political arrangements are in place. Not only would such a settlement be a major element in securing that stability in the Southeast Asian region which is itself a major Australian interest, but it could be helpful in further developing Australia's political and trade relations with China.

In Northeast Asia Australia is, of necessity, more of an observer than a participant. That Australia is interested in peace on the Korean peninsula, and a peaceful transition in North Korea to an effective and more outward-looking post-Kim-Il-sung regime is obvious. With China there is, equally clearly, not a great deal of effective business to be done until the shape, and the policies, of the post-Deng period become clearer. And perhaps not even then if, as seems quite possible, China's internal confusions and constraints persist. The way in which China's attitudes, even now, are leading to the running down of Hong Kong does not encourage optimism.

There remains the matter of Japan. From an Australian point of view the issues here concern not just the Pacific balance of political and military power, but vital questions of Australia's external trade, payments, and investment. Like a number of other countries around the Pacific, Australia is much more wary than the United States of any major additional expansion of Japanese military power. Not just because of its strategic consequences, but because of the possible political effects within Japan. Within that context, the role of Japanese forces in the defense of Japan, in partially protecting some Pacific sea-lanes, and in operating in close conjunction with the United States and its allies is, of course, welcome. But the spectacle of Japanese policymaking difficulties with respect to the Gulf affair, and the difficulties this has caused in relations between Tokyo and Washington, will be closely watched in Canberra. So will the domestic political difficulties the affair has caused for the Japanese government. Altogether, the evidence of a marked discrepancy between Japanese economic might, and Japan's ability and willingness to play any corresponding external political role, is likely to lead to some reappraisals in Canberra. Arguably of even greater importance is the role of Japan in Australia's economic life.

That life has a number of characteristics which are important for any understanding of Australia's external policies. Australia has, over half a century or more, built up a secondary manufacturing sector which was, and to some extent still is, well protected and inward looking. But Australia has, at the same time, consistently relied on overseas sources for a large range of goods and services as well as capital for the nation's development. The required export income has been derived,

AUSTRALIA'S STRATEGIC INTEREST   179

for some decades, in a rough 40:40:20 ratio from raw materials, farm produce, and manufacturing and service exports. Downturns in international market prices for commodities and/or food are apt to have, and have had, quite severe consequences for Australia and her balance of payments, which is currently in deficit to the tune of around $A20 billion per annum.

In looking to the future, Australia's economic planners do not, so far, seem to foresee any quick or marked expansion of exports of goods and services. They have tended to focus rather more on such factors as Australia's potential ability to associate with the more rapidly growing economies of the Western Pacific and, most especially, to sell Australia's efficiently produced foodstuffs to the populations of the Asian fringe, which demographic projections suggest will grow much more rapidly than will their ability to feed themselves.

Some attention has also been paid to the future patterns suggested by observers like Kenichi Ohmae, who has seen global economic developments partly in terms of three linked groupings: one centered upon Europe and including parts of Africa, one centered upon the United States and comprising the Americas, and one centered upon Japan and including much of East and Southeast Asia. It is possible to question such pattern-making. The evidence is strong that in such groupings as ASEAN, or even the European Community, some members have "external" economic (and political) interests which are at least as important to them as their interests within the group. Nevertheless, Australians have thought hard about the extent to which their economic future might lie within an Asian grouping of which Japan would be the economically most powerful member. At the same time, recent figures suggest that Australia's most important economic partners remain the United States and Europe, together with Japan, and that the United States and Europe are of special importance in investment flows.

In the years 1987–88 to 1989–90, Australia's merchandise and commodity exports rose from $A41.0 to $A49.1 billions, while imports rose from $A40.5 to $A51.3 billions. Within those totals exports to the European Community rose from

$A6.4 to $A6.8 billions and imports from $A9.7 to $A11.3 billions. Exports to the United States went up from $A4.6 to $A5.3 billions and imports from $A8.5 to $A12.3 billions. In the case of Japan, Australian exports rose from $A10.7 to $A12.8 billions and imports from $A7.8 to $A9.8 billions. Consequently, while Japan was Australia's largest single export market, as a source of imports both the United States and Europe were more important, and seem likely to remain so.

The pattern of investment flows is no less revealing. Between 1986–87 and 1988–89 total foreign investment in Australia rose from $A139.4 billion to $A195.6 billion, while Australian investment abroad rose from $A43.2 to $A72.5 billions. Within those totals, US investment in Australia went up from $A4.6 to $A5.9 billions, EC investment declined from $A5.3 to $A4.0 billions and Japanese investment ballooned from $A814 millions to $A4.7 billions. But by the end of 1988–89 the levels of foreign investment in Australia showed that the European Community was much the largest investor, with a total of $A66.9 billions (the United Kingdom alone holding investments of $A47.1 billions), followed by the United States with $A46.8 billions and Japan with $A33.3 billions. Conversely, much the greatest total of Australian foreign investment was concentrated in the United States, with $A32.5 billions, followed by the EC with $A17.9 billions (United Kingdom: $A13.8 billions), followed by New Zealand with $A5.5 billions, and only then Japan which has Australian investments of $A4.4 billions.

It seems reasonable to conclude that Australia's trade and investment ties will continue to be highly diversified across the globe rather than concentrated in any one or two geographical areas. That view seems supported not just by the general globalization of technology and financial flows in the current period but by the obvious desirability, for all advanced states, of diversifying markets and sources of supply in an uncertain world so as to be less dependent upon any single source of economic or, for that matter, political support.

THE CHANGING PACIFIC STRATEGIC ENVIRONMENT

Ross Cottrill

Mr. Ross W. Cottrill *graduated with first class honors from Sydney University. He has also attended the Australian National University, Hong Kong, and George Washington Universities. He has been head of the Department of Foreign Affairs' policy planning unit, counselor at the Australian Embassy in Washington, and from 1979–80 held a senior position in the Department of the Prime Minister. Mr. Cottrill then joined the Department of Defence and was responsible for strategic and defense policy matters. Mr. Cottrill's division managed the Defence Cooperation Program and policy for the international relations of the defense organization. After completing the advanced management program at Harvard University he headed the International Policy Division and was then appointed Special Adviser to the Secretary and the Chief of the Defence Force.*

The nations of the Pacific include two of the three largest concentrations of economic power in the world. The United States has the largest economy in the world, and Japan achieved, during the four decades to 1990, the most rapid peacetime improvement in relative economic status in recorded history. Pacific nations also have the largest and most powerful armed forces in the world: those of the United States, the Soviet Union, China, the Democratic People's Republic of Korea and Republic of Korea, as well as Vietnam and Japan.

Forces shaping the Pacific environment of the future are more than ever global. The kinds of questions which are involved in the Pacific have to do with the implications of the sudden end of Cold War confrontation in Europe and its implications for the pattern of power relationships. The easing of strategic competition could open the way for some new order, whether this is the New International Order or some other system in which strategic equilibrium would be less dependent than in the past on military power and where international institutions might have a more substantial decisionmaking role. The extent to which US military burdens might be lightened, its national priorities readjusted, and its external commitments reduced by encouraging more self-reliance on the part of allies and those who have relied on the United States in the past are all relevant to the future of the Pacific, as well as globally.

After the Cold War

The end of the Cold War has relaxed tensions in the Pacific. The United States and the Soviet Union have been able to work together constructively on a wide range of issues, including some major arms control issues, and the overall climate of international relations has improved. The Soviet Union and The Republic of Korea have substantially improved their communications. Vietnam and China have been able to do business on Cambodian issues, and tensions between them seem to be easing.

There is no parallel in the Pacific with the dramatic changes in Europe where a series of communist regimes in the east collapsed, where the failure of command economies has been widely accepted, and *glasnost* has revealed the emptiness of communist ideology. These changes and the demise of the Warsaw Pact have closed off the threat of a massive Soviet ground force attack being mounted at short notice against Western Europe.

Military confrontation with the Soviet Union during the Cold War was not as concentrated in the Pacific, and the break with the past has not been as sharp. There has been no equivalent of NATO as a permanent multilateral alliance with integrated forces in place. Although containment and deterrence of the Soviet Union were unifying threads running through US management of its alliances in the Pacific, the threat perceptions of its various alliance partners and associates have been more diverse. China and Japan have seen the Soviet Union as their principal source of threat. South Korea and North Korea have each perceived the other as a source of threat. Vietnam perceives China as its principal threat; some of its Southeast Asian neighbors sense pressure from Vietnam and have some concern about China and Japan in the longer term. Among the less militarily powerful South East Asian countries, internal security is typically a higher priority than external threats. And for the small Pacific island countries "security" and national independence tend to be seen as threatened more by factors such as geographical remoteness, economic dependence, and vulnerability to undesirable non-state actors, than by military power.

Partnership, Cooperation, or Competition

In an earlier period, concepts were developed to emphasize the kinds of changes that détente could bring. Commentators spoke of a shift from bipolar to multipolar patterns of power; of the diffusion of power among a larger number of states; and of the changing nature of power. There was recognition of growing economic interdependence and of the intertwining of security and economic relationships. They are still relevant, but they do not seem to take us far enough in explaining the nature and scale of the changes we now see. The roles of both the Soviet Union and the United States are now subject to change in a way that was inconceivable during the Cold War. In assessing prospects for the future, therefore, we need to identify the more enduring factors.

The Soviet Union will be such a major, continuing factor in the Pacific. It remains a formidable, nuclear power; it still has potent conventional military forces. Its ideological appeal has faded away. In future, it will depend on combining its military power with effective diplomacy and on the extent to which it can widen its appeal beyond traditional security issues. Internal pressures are the main determinants of change in the Soviet role in the Pacific. The Baltic republics and some of the Asian republics of the Union could eventually gain autonomy or even formal independence. Their struggles toward these objectives could have reverberations which would affect neighboring states. The pressures are so great that the disintegration of the Union, or the substitution of some looser confederation are real possibilities. These internal changes could lead to tensions with the Soviet Union's neighbors, including China, and could make more difficult the eventual emergence of a stable regime with democratic institutions and an economic system which its citizens would accept as offering a reasonable standard of living. Concerns such as these could lead to a need for the "strategic" use of economic aid and other assistance to moderate pressures within the Soviet Union.

It is the Slavic heartland of the Soviet Union which in the event of some republics being lost from the Union is likely—either in the name of the USSR or as successor state—to control the Soviet military machine. It is, therefore, the debates centered in Moscow which will have the more far-reaching effects for the Pacific.

Soviet political life is dominated by vigorous competition for influence between those who want to reform economic and political structures more rapidly and those who give priority to retaining structures of power and control. Though Soviet leaders are preoccupied with internal affairs, foreign policy has itself become an area in dispute between reformers and traditionalists. The latter are prepared to pay a greater price in terms of foregoing cooperation with the United States in order to pursue nationalist interests.

While such fundamental issues remain unresolved in Moscow, Soviet external policy will be much less predictable than it has been in the past. And we do not know how long resolution will take. With reformers ascendant, there could be opportunities to integrate the Soviet Union with the community of developed nations. But until reformers have firm control of the institutions of state power; until there is a functioning democratic system, and prospects of economic progress to blunt the appeals of nationalism, there will remain a risk of reversion to harsher external policies.

Notwithstanding this new unpredictability in Soviet politics, the potential military threat posed by the Soviet Union is reduced in several respects. The disastrous state of the economy would tend to discourage new, large-scale, external undertakings. The Afghanistan experience and the inglorious withdrawals from Eastern Europe have undermined the prestige of Soviet military might. With a lesser proportion of the Soviet navy ranging far afield, and Moscow's capacity to provide economic assistance curtailed, it is less able to project power beyond areas adjacent to its own territory. Its nuclear potential will continue to require deterrence by the United States and, through its alliance system, the United States will provide extended deterrence to its various allies.

Stabilizing the Balance

As an objective of policy "stability" has always had appeal. It seems to threaten no one, and promises a minimum of surprises. In the Pacific of the future, however, change within nations is to be expected, and in cases where it moves in the direction of more democratic political systems and market economy it could be beneficial. Changes of the kind in prospect within the Soviet Union will impact on the structure of the balance among major powers in ways we cannot usefully predict. In the face of such pressures, policy can be "stabilizing" in that it seeks to dampen adverse repercussions, but does not attempt to guarantee "stability."

The United States will continue to have a balancing role, by virtue of its military "edge," its breadth of diplomatic access, its political prestige and its economic capacity. The nature of the role will be clear, but nations do not always pursue their interests. The United States might seek to shift more of its effort to the pursuit of interests other than strategic ones. There is now more room for choice by the United States as to how actively it wishes to play this balancing role and whether it wishes to share leadership in the Pacific with Japan.

The predominant pattern of relationships among the major powers in the Pacific is loosely multipolar with a tendency to become looser over time, as the Soviet Union and the United States adjust to the end of the Cold War and the circle of participants tends to widen. The multipolar dimension of the balance is demonstrated clearly in relation to the security on the Korean peninsula. While principally involving the two Korean parties themselves, it also engages major interests of Japan, China, and the Soviet Union as well as the United States. This multilateral pattern has been reflected in consensus among these powers on some Korean issues in the past and could assist continued progress toward Korean reunification.

The crucial question of the security of Japan involves the interests of a wider grouping. While constitutional provisions inhibit military development for other than self-defence purposes, Japan's military capabilities are continuing to grow, with the active encouragement of the United States. Japan remains firmly allied with the United States. Regional neighbors are wary of Japan's military potential, yet value the US-Japan alliance as an essential component of the regional balance. The development of military capabilities for the defense of Japan is accepted regionally in the context of the US-Japan alliance—while the alliance is working effectively and the forces of the two countries are working in close conjunction. Japan eschews any regional security role. It is for this reason that, from time to time, attacks on the Japanese alliance in the United States send ripples quite widely through the Pacific.

China's role is likely to change during the decade. Its role in the US-Soviet-China triangle faded with *perestroika* and the development of US-Soviet cooperation. The faltering of its drive for modernization and the events of *Tienanmen* weakened its ties with the West and its focus turned inward. The pressure to modernize the economy and its defense capacity will, however, keep up pressure for greater access to Western investment, technology, and markets. China could thus resume a more active role internationally, but the enduring problem of its security vis-à-vis the Soviet Union will maintain its orientation in the power balance.

In Southeast Asia, the dominant security issue has been and continues to be Cambodia. Parties external to Cambodia, including Vietnam and China, seem to generally accept that a settlement cannot be achieved by military means and that a broad consensus will be needed to support a settlement. The Permanent Five members of the Security Council have played active diplomatic roles. There has been a revival of international conference diplomacy, at varying levels of formality, and active consultations with Indonesia, Vietnam, and other Asian neighbors of Cambodia. These participants are not of similar weight and some have been facilitators rather than principals, but the interactions have been wider and more varied than the multipolar pattern would suggest and will probably continue to be while the Cambodian issue is actively pursued.

Several factors could lead to particular regional issues in future attracting a wider range of protagonists. US withdrawal from unnecessary entanglements at the regional level to concentrate more on stabilizing the wider balance could work in this direction. The emergence of issues such as the proliferation of nuclear, biological, and chemical weapon capabilities and missile technologies, which are essentially multilateral issues at the global level, can be addressed at the regional level as well. And, finally, changes in the economic priorities of both large and small Pacific countries are changing the basis of existing strategic relationships.

Economic Challenges

With the end of the Cold War it was widely expected that there would be a shift of emphasis from defense to economic issues. The Gulf crisis has interrupted this process of reorientation, but cannot reverse it. After a long period of economic growth, employment creation, and deregulation, the US economy is now in recession. That recession can be expected to sharpen the focus on the relative economic position of the United States compared with Japan. Over the last four decades the growth of Japan's economy has brought about the most rapid rise ever in relative economic status of any nation. The United States has for years had a large bilateral trade deficit with Japan. The reasons are complex and have to do with savings rates (in recent years 20.3 percent for Japan and 4.2 percent for the United States), which are related to the cost of capital to business, and investment performance (24 percent of its GNP for Japan and 10 percent for the United States. Explanations involve structural characteristics of the two economies, and management and industrial relations practices, as well as cultural patterns and language barriers. My purpose here is not to account for the differences, but to suggest some implications they have for the Pacific strategic environment.

Its economic strengths give Japan increasing economic power. Its investments in the United States have grown strongly in the 1980s and the market share of Japanese companies, particularly in electronics, has steadily increased. Japan has shown an ability to concentrate on emerging technologies which can be exploited in markets with high elasticity of demand. The growth of its production capacity in these areas gives it continuing trade leverage. And if such trends continued, even US defense industry could, in time, become dependent on Japanese technology for some components of its sophisticated weapons.

Though firm strategic allies and economically interdependent, Japan and the United States are fierce rivals commercially. Their companies compete for promising new technologies. Japanese success is perceived as threatening the future economic well-being of the United States. The rising status of Japan as an economic power increases Japan's influence at a time when the United States is newly conscious of its economic limits and vulnerabilities. The problem of the US trade deficit is far larger than the effects of Japan's restraints on trade, however. It has to do with the balance between savings and consumption which is also basic to the problem of the

US fiscal deficit. Movement by the United States toward over-all balance in its overseas trade with a stronger performance in savings as compared with consumption would relieve some of the pressures in its dealings with Japan. But the most potent reason for making this shift would be to improve the long-run economic performance of the United States itself.

Market access is an issue between the United States and Japan, but the issue is much broader than that. Friction caused by restraints on market access and export subsidies has been growing strongly in recent years. The active trading nations of the world have been continuing to enlarge the markets to which they have assured or preferred access. The European Economic Community, North America, and Japan are the centers around which contending trade blocs could develop with each limiting access by non-members to its own bloc. There have been suggestions that East and Southeast Asian countries might form such a bloc with Japan. With General Agreement on Tariffs and Trade (GATT) negotiations in the Uruguay Round at an impasse and currently suspended, tensions between major trading nations are at a high point.

How do these economic forces affect strategic considerations? This is difficult to answer without suggesting that we have considered security issues too narrowly in the past. Economic growth is impaired by restraint of trade and growth foregone means less resources available for defense. But after the Cold War, and assuming tensions continue to be relaxed, defense will probably have less call on available resources, with or without impairment of growth prospects. Some of the nations contending over trade and economic issues are actively cooperating in response to the Gulf crisis. But when the Gulf crisis is past, support for alliances and other commitments comes under pressure—in democratic countries—and commitments become more questionable while economic tensions persist. In the more fluid environment of the Pacific in the future, security is less likely to be an overriding priority, and beyond a certain minimum provision for national self-defense in the context of their immediate vicinity, states will tend to constrain defense spending sharply, and give priority to improving their economic well-being.

Alliances and Coalition Diplomacy

Changes in power relativities are likely to be accentuated by the Gulf War. It is a test of US commitment and confidence; the need to escape the "Vietnam syndrome" is being stressed repeatedly. Success in the Gulf will be measured essentially in terms of time and costs, and the stabilization of the region after the war is over. If the United States itself does not feel that the results are worth the cost, there would be risk of it turning inward and reducing foreign entanglements. The success which has been achieved on the battlefield should mean that the United States can put behind it the "Vietnam syndrome", the "decline" thesis, and the specter of the pitiable, bound giant.

Two further issues are raised by US involvement in the Gulf. Even if the economic costs are offset largely by financial contributions, the United States will be reluctant to risk such a major military role again on behalf of the international community. Nor are similar circumstances likely to arise again: Iraq's was an extreme case. Security priorities will need to be rigorously reexamined. Thresholds will need to be identified, and planning developed so that security needs can be met, with the means that can be expected realistically to be available for such purposes.

The alliances which the United States has in the Pacific are generally bilateral, rather than multilateral like NATO. There is thus more flexibility and capacity to adapt to change. Such adaptation has occurred in the past. In the case of Australia, the source threat against which the Australia, New Zealand, United States (ANZUS) Treaty was to guarantee Australia was seen in the 1950s to be Japan. Those notions have long since faded and Australia in more recent times has preferred not to base its planning on any identified threat, but has seen ANZUS as a means of supporting the United States and the Western community of nations generally in their strategic competition with the Soviet Union and its associates.

Responses to the Gulf crisis have involved several elements of what has been termed the New International Order. The role of the United Nations Security Council has been crucial in applying fundamental principles, determining how they have been violated, and defining the purposes of collective security action. A second crucial element has been the role of the United States as coalition leader in harnessing diplomacy and military responsibility together, and guiding the military effort of the coalition. There was no alternative, even though the UN has provision for a Military Staff Committee comprising the Chiefs of Staff of the Five Permanent members of the Security Council, each having the right to veto. It would be unrealistic to expect the United States or any other major power to submit its military planning to the direction or oversight of this committee. Thus, not only in the Gulf, but also in other cases where Security Council decisions require substantial military measures, it would be for the United States to play the leading military role. If the United States were reluctant to play the role of international policeman, and UN collectively is not presently structured for the role, who then will do it?

A third factor has been the emergence of burden-sharing as a major issue, notwithstanding the assembling of a broad coalition which includes those formally allied to the United States as well as many that are formally nonaligned. Allies who had suitable forces and were not subject to particular constraints were expected to contribute. Allies who are not contributing militarily in the Gulf are making substantial financial contributions. The experience of having financial contributions levied and paid on this scale raises the possibility that similar approaches could in time be developed in a scaled-down version to meet regional needs in the Pacific.

Regionalism and the New Order

If tensions and competition between the United States and the Soviet Union continue to diminish, it might be expected that there could be increased scope for regional structures and institutions. For the United States there could be advantage in allowing regional countries to find their own level and to reduce US burdens.

The Pacific does not really function as a single region in strategic terms, however. Apart from the North American nations, the Pacific has several regional focuses of which the strongest is the security of Japan and Korea. In Southeast Asia there is ASEAN and the Indo-China group. The central and southern Pacific islands, Australia, and New Zealand meet for regional political consultations in the Pacific Forum. There are growing patterns of bilateral consultations and networks to deal with specialist and technical issues, but there is no institutional framework to cover strategic issues in the Pacific as a whole. Improved consultations among regional countries on security issues are needed, perhaps beginning in an informal way and drawing in academic and nonofficial networks.

Within ASEAN there is an awareness that Cambodia is the central issue on which they have concentrated their efforts for some years. If and when there is a settlement, ASEAN would need another focus. In recent years there has been discussion of a "core" group of Indonesia, Malaysia, and Singapore. This group of countries works more closely together in developing and sharing their perceptions of long-term security interests; their economic circumstances and prospects are now more closely related; and they have committed themselves to a "growth triangle" which would eventually give them a substantial economic stake in a collective venture.

For the smaller and more remote states of the Pacific the end of the Cold War and related adjustments are likely to reduce one of the motivations—competition for influence—supporting development assistance. Freer and more multilateral patterns of interaction are not likely to benefit all regional countries equally. The smaller and less influential are thus likely to need to work harder at maintaining their access to investment, trade, and technology, as well as for support on security-related matters.

Commitments and Presence

The Gulf crisis has seen the United States assemble and lead a massive coalition force, and use it with dramatic effect. The massive power needed to deal with the Iraqi invasion is likely to create apprehension in some areas that the United States might be inclined to interventionism and to imposing its will by force. This would be an unnecessary concern, both because there is no cause in the Pacific which could trigger the formation of such a forceful coalition, and because the United States will be reluctant to expend such effort again for quite a long time.

Economic pressures will oblige the United States to be more sparing of its commitments in the future. Those pressures are likely to result in further reductions in US defense effort and a more selective identification of interests which could appropriately be supported by military means. There will be more reliance on indirect means—on political influence, economic adjustments, and diplomacy—to support security generally and to afford substantial protection for particular US interests.

Provided the current round of negotiations with the Philippines is successful, facilities at Subic Bay and Clark Field will be available to the United States until around the end of the decade. But the course of those negotiations has obliged both the United States and its regional partners to consider directly the end of the permanent US military presence in Southeast Asia. Such withdrawal has become a real possibility. With the Soviet departure from Cam Ranh Bay, there is thus a possibility, around the end of the 1990s, of there being *no* superpower military presence ashore in Southeast Asia. Despite the regional wariness expressed over the years, there is some unease as to what this change would mean, not so much in the short term but in relation to the emergence of China, Japan, and India as increasingly active powers with potential for rivalry at least at the diplomatic and political levels. Apart from the Five Power Defence Arrangements, the region does not have multilateral systems to support regional security. Networks of bilateral cooperation are growing steadily, but further development of consultation and cooperation requires priority attention.

Korea is an area where further reductions can be made, having regard to progress in the reunification of North and South Korea, and the attitudes and likely reactions of interested powers especially Japan, China, and the Soviet Union. The US presence in support of the security of Japan is in a different category. The United States is the only power which can deter the nuclear component of any Soviet threat to Japan; and its involvement there on a substantial scale has a wider stabilizing influence in the region. The US presence and practical cooperation with the Japanese Self-Defence Force demonstrate and sustain Japan's strategic linkage with the United States.

Future Balance in the Pacific

The Pacific has not felt the effects of the end of the Cold War as dramatically and directly as the Atlantic, but tensions have been reduced. A major element of uncertainty stems from internal pressures in the Soviet Union, which will make it difficult to predict the role to be played by the Soviet Union, or its successor state, in the future. In particular, the balance to be struck between partnership and competition with the United States is unclear. However, Soviet capacity for the projection of power and influence will be reduced and deterrence of Soviet military pressure is likely to focus more sharply on Japan.

The balance in the Pacific has been described as "loosely multilateral" and it seems likely to become looser as we move through the decade. The US military "edge" over other powers has increased and the United States could be inclined to define its priorities more sharply, reducing its regional entanglements. Other factors working in this direction are the possibility of China again becoming more outward-looking and internationally active, and the claims of some proliferation issues which require international attention.

Economic challenges are forcing changes in the structure of the economies of the United States and Japan *inter alia*. This process is necessary to allow the US-Japan alliance to remain vital, to accommodate the increasing economic interdependence between them, and to fend off the prospect of trade wars which would hurt all of us. Burden-sharing has taken on a new life in the Gulf crisis and we can expect some carrying over into the Pacific. There are likely to be further reductions in the US military presence abroad, but with Japan recognized as a special and crucially important case.

ABOUT THE EDITOR . . .

Dr. Dora Alves is a South Pacific specialist and an editor, NDU Press. Dr. Alves was born in England and educated at St. Anne's College, Oxford University. She holds graduate degrees from American University and the Catholic University of America. As a naval analyst she has specialized in Australia, New Zealand, and the Pacific area where she has traveled and lectured. Dr. Alves lectures at the National War College and the Inter-American Defense College, and has been director of the Industrial College of the Armed Forces' security studies for Southeast Asia, Australia, and the Philippines. She is the author of The ANZUS Partners, Anti-Nuclear Attitudes in New Zealand and Australia, and Defending Northern Australia (forthcoming). Her most recent articles are "Jam Today: The Troubles on Bougainville" and "The Need for Creative Naval Strategy." A book on US-Australian cooperation is in progress.